上班族必备口袋

上班族
·必备

职场会话

OFFICE TALK:
GETTING AHEAD IN THE BUSINESS WORLD

LiveABC 编著

科学出版社
北京

图字：01-2010-1595 号

本书原名《上班族必备职场会话》原出版者LiveABC Interactive Corporation，经授权由科学出版社在中国大陆地区独家出版发行。

图书在版编目（CIP）数据

上班族必备职场会话／LiveABC编著．—北京：科学出版社，2010
（上班族必备口袋书系列）
ISBN 978-7-03-027918-7

Ⅰ．①上…　Ⅱ．①L…　Ⅲ．①商业—英语—口语
Ⅳ．①H319.9

中国版本图书馆CIP数据核字（2010）第 109935 号

责任编辑：张　培／责任校对：张　琪
责任印制：赵德静／封面设计：无极书装

联系电话：010-6401 9074　　电子邮箱：zhangpei@mail.sciencep.com

斜 学 出 版 社 出版
北京东黄城根北街16号
邮政编码：100717
http://www.sciencep.com

骏 杰 印 刷 厂 印刷
科学出版社发行　　各地新华书店经销

*

2010 年 9 月第 一 版　　开本：787×960 1/32
2010 年 9 月第一次印刷　　印张：11 3/8
字数：324 000

定价：25.00 元（含 1 张 MP3 光盘）
（如有印装质量问题，我社负责调换）

前　言

　　随着经济全球化的来临，用一种共通的语言与不同国家的人士沟通，已成为一种必然的趋势，而英语正是大多数人的选择。

　　随着国际贸易日渐频繁，较具规模的公司也常聘用一些外国人，即使是一般的上班族也随时有可能需要和来自世界各国的客户交流。只有拥有良好的英语能力，才能顺利地表达自己的意见，和外国同事沟通协调，使彼此在工作中愉快合作。目前各大公司对员工外语能力的要求越来越高，在激烈竞争的职场中，熟悉职场英语会话绝对是不可或缺的技能，这不但是应届毕业生求职时的加分要件，更是在职人员需要重点掌握的技能。

　　《上班族必备职场会话》一书的背景是以一家电子公司"太阳科技"的企业活动场景为主线，大致分为9大主题，包括"新人守则"、"基本工作"、"闲暇聊天"、"在职培训"等不同的工作场合，把上班族可能面对的各种情况归纳起来，展现各种情境下的实用英语对话。例如：应届毕业生找工作、应聘、面试时常用的英语，还有录用后向同事请教、学习使用办公设备等适应新工作时的对话，或是接电话、记录电话留言时的电话用语。同时，通过太阳科技公司同事间的互动，介绍早退、请假、加薪、发奖金、辞职、退休甚至解雇等行政和人事变动时常用的会话。另外本书还归纳了公司内部进行产品营销、商务简报、讨论议题时常见的会议用语。而对外方面则涵盖和客户约定会面、介绍商品、处理订单、议价、参加商务招待会、安排出差等林林总总的情况，从而使读者学到全面而实用的职场英语。

全书共有 56 个单元，在每个单元首页都精心设计了主题重点摘要，有些是针对每个单元的情境主题介绍相关的职场信息，例如：简历的写作要点、面试的诀窍、上下班的注意事项等；有些则是分条列出相关的中英名词对照，例如：公司里常见的各种职称或是部门分类等，让读者对职场英语的相关知识或信息有更广泛的认识。本书由美籍教师编写以生动的对话呈现出鲜活的情境，用字遣词自然流畅。在英语会话范例中，列举出了对话中较难理解的单词或短语，加注 KK 音标，使读者能准确发音，并提供中文翻译，使读者学起来轻松又容易。而在学习重点部分，我们从对话中挑选常用的单词短语加以说明，补充相似用语或其他用法，并提供例句，使读者学得更加全面透彻。

本书提供原文朗读 MP3，还设计了听力小测验，帮助您练习听力。这是一本实用的英语口语书籍，希望通过不同主题的分册，帮助读者提升英语会话能力。

如何使用本书

本书分为**9**大主题共**56**个单元，包括"新人守则"、"报到日"、"基本工作"、"闲暇聊天"、"客户至上"、"争取权益"、"在职培训"、"危机处理"、"重要会议"，并提供原文朗读MP3，还设计了听力小测验，帮助您练习听力，英语学得轻松又容易。

新人守则   UNIT 01

找工作
SEARCHING FOR A JOB

简历构成的5大要素

résumé指"简历"，是向雇佣单位陈述其经历的文件，也可称作resume。在美式英语中又称为CV（curriculum），一般的英文简历是以条列形式的方式介绍个人背景、专长的内容包括：

① 联系方式（contact information）
② 教育背景（education）
③ 工作经历（employment history）
④ 奖励荣誉（honors and awards）
⑤ 特殊技能（special skills）

简历一般还包括求职者本人隐私的信息（privacy），通常不列个人资料，如生日（date of birth）、婚姻状况（marital status）、兴趣（hobbies），以及身高、体重、血型等信息不必列出。另外，简历结尾常写上一行references available upon request，意指有需要将提供工作证明、学历证明，或推荐信。

第2页 TRACK 26 27-28

单元页

精心设计单元主题重点摘要，针对每个单元的情境主题介绍相关的职场信息。

英文对话范例

对话范例   有声朗诵示范

① Josie Gleason is looking for a job. She asks her friend Dave for advice.

② [情境图片]

③ Josie: Dave, what's the best way to find a job?

Dave: The want ads in the newspaper are probably a good place to start.

Josie: I've been checking the want ads every day for a week, and I can't find anything that I'm qualified for. And the few that I have seen—very low-paying.

Dave: Try the Internet. You can use a search engine to find job sites¹ related to your field.²

Josie: Great idea! Thanks! I think I'll look for something in sales.

④ 页 002   TRACK 01

Dave: Hey, I just saw a job opening in sales, at a company called Sun Tech. It could be just the sort of thing you're looking for.

Josie: Really?

Dave: Yeah, but if I remember . . . the deadline³ is this afternoon.

Josie: This afternoon?! Ahh! I'd better get on-line quickly and see if I can submit⁴ my résumé by e-mail.

Dave: Wait, have you updated⁵ your résumé? It should mention your sales experience.

Josie: Don't worry. It's all set. Thanks, buddy.

Dave: Any time, Josie.

⑥ 1. job site〔'dʒab.saɪt〕求职网站
2. field〔fild〕n. 领域、范围
3. deadline〔'dɛd.laɪn〕n. 截止时间
4. submit〔səb'mɪt〕v. 提交、递交
5. update〔ʌp'det〕v. 更新

页 003

① 内容大纲   ③ 英文对话   ⑤ 学习重点
② 情境图片   ④ 页码及MP3 对应文件   ⑥ 补充单词

中文翻译及学习重点

短语
单词

例句

单词
翻译

词语
解析

听力小测验

照片
描述

回答
问题

简短对话

目　录

重要会议

找工作
SEARCHING FOR A JOB

简历构成的**5**大要素

résumé 指 "简历"，是由法语借用过来的外来语，也可写作 resume，在英式英语中又称为 CV (curriculum)。一般的英文简历是以分条列出的方式介绍个人背景，常见的内容包括：

❶ 联系方式 (contact information)
❷ 教育背景 (education)
❸ 工作经历 (employment history)
❹ 奖励荣誉 (honors and awards)
❺ 特殊技能 (special skills)

值得一提的是，在美国因为注重隐私权 (privacy)，通常不把个人资料，如生日 (date of birth)、婚姻状况 (marital status)、兴趣 (hobbies)，以及身高、体重、血型等放在简历中。另外，简历结尾常会写上一行 references available upon request，表示能够提供工作证明、学历证明，或推荐信等。

Josie Gleason is looking for a job. She asks her friend Dave for advice.

Josie: Dave, what's the best way to find a job?

Dave: The **want ads** in the newspaper are probably a good place to start.

Josie: I've been checking the want ads every day for a week, and I can't find anything that I'm **qualified for**. And the few that I have seen—very low-paying.

Dave: Try the Internet. You can use a search engine to find job sites[1] related to your field.[2]

Josie: Great idea! Thanks! I think I'll look for something in sales.

Dave: Hey, I just saw a **job opening** in sales, at a company called Sun Tech. It could be just the sort of thing you're looking for.

Josie: Really?

Dave: Yeah, but if I remember . . . the deadline[3] is this afternoon.

Josie: This afternoon?! Ahh! I'd better get on-line quickly and see if I can submit[4] my résumé by e-mail.

Dave: Wait, have you updated[5] your résumé? It should mention your sales experience.

Josie: Don't worry. It's all set. Thanks, buddy.

Dave: Any time, Josie.

---

1. job site [ˈdʒɑbˌsaɪt] 招聘网站
2. field [fiːd] *n.* 领域；范围
3. deadline [ˈdɛdˌlaɪn] *n.* 截止时间
4. submit [səbˈmɪt] *v.* 提交；呈递
5. update [ʌpˈdet] *v.* 更新

中文翻译 TRANSLATION

乔西·格利森正在找工作。她请她朋友戴夫给她一些建议。

Josie: 戴夫，找工作什么方式最好？

Dave: 从报纸上的招聘广告开始着手应该不错。

Josie: 我每天都看招聘广告，已经看了一个星期了，还是没有看到我能胜任的工作。而少数几个我能做的嘛——薪水都很低。

Dave: 上网试试看。你可以用搜寻引擎寻找跟你专业领域相关的招聘网站。

Josie: 好主意！谢啦！我想我会找销售方面的工作。

Dave: 嘿，我刚刚看到一家叫太阳科技的公司在招销售人员。那可能正是你要找的那类工作。

Josie: 真的吗？

Dave: 是啊，但是如果我没记错……申请期限截止到今天下午。

Josie: 今天下午？！天哪！我最好赶快上网，看看是不是能用电子邮件把我的简历寄过去。

Dave: 等一下，你简历的资料更新了吗？上面应该要提到你的销售经验。

Josie: 别担心。一切都准备好了。谢啦，朋友。

Dave: 别客气，乔西。

学习重点

want ad 报纸招聘广告

ad是advertisement的缩写，通常是指刊登在报纸、杂志等平面媒体上的广告；而电视、收音机等的广告则称作commercial。一般的分类广告（classified ad）包括求助广告（Help Wanted）、出售广告（For Sale）、寻人启事（Missing Person）等。

● Our department needs more staff, so we placed a **want ad** in the paper.

我们部门需要更多的人员，所以我们在报纸上刊登了一则招聘广告。

qualified for 胜任；有资格……

qualified [ˋkwɑlɪ͵faɪd] *adj.* 胜任的；有资格的

qualified for + N. 表示"胜任（工作、职位等）"。而qualified to + V. 表示"有资格去做……"。

● Scott's knowledge of computers made him **qualified for** the position.

斯科特的电脑知识使他能胜任这个工作。

job opening 职位空缺

也常说成job vacancy。job常用来指赚钱养家、维持生活的工作（work），可分成全职的（full-time）、兼职的（part-time）、永久的（permanent）或临时性的（temporary）。"职业"的正式用语是occupation，口语中常说成line of work。

● There are plenty of **job openings** in town.

城里有许多职位空缺。

听力小测验　　　　　　　　GIVE IT A TRY!

Photographs

You will hear four statements about a picture. Choose the one statement that best describes what you see in the picture. The statements will be spoken only one time.

Ans: _____

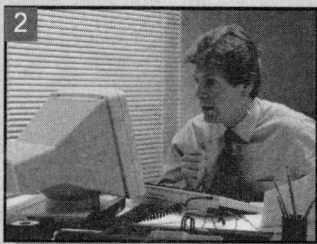

Ans: _____

Question and Response

You will hear a question or statement and three responses. Choose the best response to the question or statement. They will be spoken only one time.

1. _____ 2. _____ 3. _____ 4. _____

应聘工作
APPLYING FOR A JOB

应聘时的 **5** 大诀窍

❶ 应填完申请表格 (application forms) 所有的内容。

❷ 交表格时，要附上一份简历 (résumé)。简历最好不要
超过三页，除非你有一长串相关的工作经历。

❸ 如果准备了简历 (résumé)，记得加上一页自荐信
(cover letter)，根据所要应聘的职务，重点简述自己
相关的资格 (qualifications)，以引起审核者的注意与
兴趣。在英文里对于简历内容常用 be neat 来要求，也
就是要做到"简洁而有条理"；毕竟长篇大论，却不着
边际，倒不如一语中的更加有用。

❹ 如果亲自去应聘，记得一定要带笔，可以显得非常专
业，有能独当一面的感觉。

❺ 对于表格的内容，最重要的一点是"诚实填写"。如
果日后上司发现其中有造假的成分，是可以据此解雇
(terminate / fire) 员工的，所以千万不要在申请表上
造假！

对话范例

Josie is at Sun Tech, a large electronics company, **applying for** a job. She is talking to the receptionist[1], Diane Holstein.

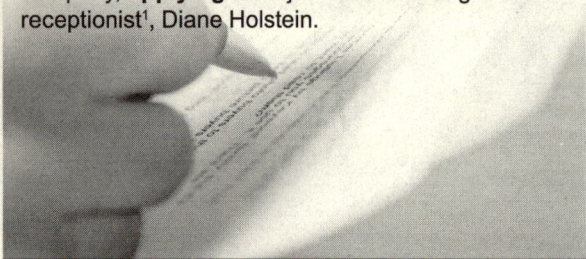

Diane: *(Into telephone)* OK, Mr. Jones. We'll talk to you soon. Bye-bye.

Josie: Good morning. I saw your Internet ad for a salesperson. I'd like to apply for the job.

Diane: OK, then. Please **fill in** this application. Use blue or black ink and write in **capital letters**.

Josie: OK. I have my résumé with me.

Diane: Great. I'll attach[2] it to your application form when you're done. Have a seat.

(Later . . .)

Josie: Excuse me, madam. I have a question.

Diane: Yes, what can I help you with?

Josie: What should I write here if I don't have any awards[3] or professional organizations[4] to list?

Diane: Just leave that part blank.

Josie: OK. I think I've filled everything in correctly. When can I expect to hear from you?

Diane: After we review your résumé, we'll call and let you know if we want you to come in for an interview.[5]

Josie: Great. Thank you very much.

Diane: You're welcome. Have a good day.

Josie: Thank you.

---

1. receptionist [rɪˋsɛpʃənɪst] *n.* 接待人员
2. attach [əˋtætʃ] *v.* 附在……上
3. award [əˋwɔrd] *n.* 奖项；奖品；奖金
4. professional organization [prəˋfɛʃənl ͵ɔrgənəˋzeʃən] 专业机构
5. interview [ˋɪntə͵vju] *n.* 面试；面谈

中文翻译   **TRANSLATION**

乔西到一家叫做太阳科技的大型电子公司应聘。她正在和前台黛安·荷尔斯坦交谈。

Diane: （对电话说）好的，琼斯先生，我们会很快和你联络，再见。

Josie: 早上好。我看到你们网络上的广告在招销售员。我想应聘这个职务。

Diane: 好的，那么请填写一下这份表格。请用蓝笔或黑笔填写，并使用大写字母。

Josie: 好的。我带了我的简历。

Diane: 很好。等你填好，我会把它附在你的表格上。请坐。

（稍后……）

Josie: 不好意思，小姐。我有个问题。

Diane: 好的，什么问题？

Josie: 如果我没有任何奖励或荣誉或在专业机构工作的经历，这里我该填什么？

Diane: 空着就好了。

Josie: 好，我想我每项都填好了。你们什么时候会给我消息？

Diane: 我们看过你的简历之后会打电话通知你，看需不需要你过来面试。

Josie: 好极了，非常谢谢你。

Diane: 不客气，祝你有个愉快的一天。

Josie: 谢谢。

学习重点

apply for 申请；应聘

除了文中的 apply for a job（应聘工作）、apply for the position（应聘职务）外，常见的还有 apply for a loan（申请贷款）、apply for a scholarship（申请奖学金）和 apply for admission（入学申请）等。

- If you want to sell alcohol in your restaurant, you need to **apply for** a liquor license first.

  如果你想在餐厅里出售酒类饮品，需要先申请酒类经销执照。

fill in 填写（表格等）

fill in 常与空格（blank）连用，表示填好某一空格或某一行。而 fill out 通常指填写完整的表格（form）或问卷（questionnaire）。

- After **filling out** the survey, you will receive a free gift.

  填完这份问卷之后，你就可以得到一份免费的礼物。

- You forgot to **fill in** this box.

  你忘了填这个表格。

capital letters 大写字母

大写字母也称作 upper case；而小写字母则为 lower case。在填表或登记时常会要求使用大写字母。此外，也常会要求填表者使用印刷体（block letters）填写。

- Please write your name in **capital letters** at the bottom of this form.

  请于此表下方，用大写写出您的姓名。

听力小测验　　　　　　　　GIVE IT A TRY!

Photographs

You will hear four statements about a picture. Choose the one statement that best describes what you see in the picture. The statements will be spoken only one time.

Ans: _____

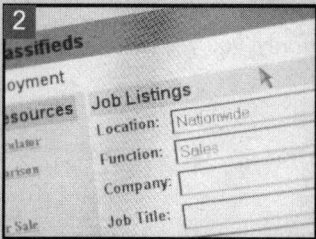

Ans: _____

Question and Response

You will hear a question or statement and three responses. Choose the best response to the question or statement. They will be spoken only one time.

1. _____ 2. _____ 3. _____ 4. _____

准备面试
PREPARING FOR AN INTERVIEW

面谈时的**6**大注意事项

❶ 穿着正式而端庄（formal and conservative）。

❷ 不要穿全新的鞋（brand-new shoes），因为新鞋常会磨脚而感到不舒服，可能会影响临场表现。

❸ 千万不要迟到。如果可能的话，至少提前 15 分钟到达，除了给人以良好的第一印象外，也可以让自己先理好思绪，避免慌乱误事。

❹ 多准备几份简历，可以当面交给面试你的人。

❺ 多问一些与公司（company）和职务（position）相关的问题，甚至包括与这个职务相关团队的人数、合作情况等细节，以显示自己想要积极地了解并争取这份工作。

❻ 不要问工作时间（working hours）、假期时间（vacation days）或薪资（pay）的问题，而是利用这次机会使对方留下深刻的印象；如果谈得融洽愉快，对方一定会主动告知或询问相关细节。

对话范例   DIALOGUE

Josie is getting ready to go to a job interview at Sun Tech. She is asking her friend Dave for some advice.

Josie: Dave, do you have any tips for a successful interview?

Dave: Well, first of all, you need to **dress professionally**.

Josie: OOh. What about during the interview?

Dave: OK, be sure to make good **eye contact**, and answer all questions politely[1] and positively.[2]

Josie: But I'm not sure what kind of questions they'll ask.

Dave: They'll probably want to know a little bit about your work experience,[3] as well as something about your character.[4]

Josie: What kind of questions should I ask them?

Dave: You should ask about the job requirements,[5] and learn a little about the company.

Josie: Should I ask about salary and working hours and vacations?

Dave: No. Not unless they **bring** it **up**. Just use the first interview to sell yourself.

Josie: You're right. If they are interested in hiring[6] me, there will be plenty of chances to talk about that later.

Dave: Right. And the more interested they are, the more they'll offer.

---

1. politely [pəˈlaɪtlɪ] *adv.* 有礼貌地
2. positively [ˈpɑzətɪvlɪ] *adv.* 明确地；肯定地
3. work experience [ˈwɜk ɪkˈspɪrɪəns] 工作经验
4. character [ˈkærɪktə] *n.* 性格；人品
5. job requirement [ˈdʒɑb ɹɪkwaɪrmənt] 工作要求
6. hire [haɪr] *v.* 雇用

中文翻译   TRANSLATION

乔西正准备要去太阳科技面试。她请她朋友戴夫提供一些建议。

Josie: 戴夫，你有没有什么面试成功的诀窍？

Dave: 嗯，首先，你得穿得正式。

Josie: 哦。那面试的时候呢？

Dave: 嗯，眼睛一定要好好看着主考官，回答问题时要有礼貌，答案要明确。

Josie: 但是我不确定他们会问我什么样的问题。

Dave: 他们可能会想知道一点你的工作经验以及你的个性如何。

Josie: 那我又该问他们什么问题？

Dave: 你应该问工作上有什么要求，并多了解这家公司。

Josie: 我应该问到薪水、工作时间和休假的事吗？

Dave: 别问，除非他们自己提起。只要利用第一次面试推销自己就好。

Josie: 你说的对。如果他们有意要雇用我，以后要谈的机会多的是。

Dave: 对啊。而且他们对你愈有兴趣，给你的薪水就会愈高。

学习重点

dress professionally 穿得正式

professionally [prə`fɛʃənlɪ] *adv.* 专业地

指穿着时，我们通常不会说"专业的穿着"，而会说"正式的穿着"。一般正式穿着的关键是：穿西装或套装（suit）、男性要打领带（tie/necktie）、穿西装裤（dress pants）、衬衫要熨烫（pressed shirt）、皮鞋要擦亮（shined shoes），其他如发型、化妆等一定要精心打理，就不必多说了。

- My father always **dresses professionally**.
  我父亲总是穿得很正式。

eye contact 目光接触

contact [`kɑntækt] *n.* 接触；交会

eye contact 的意思是指"与对方目光交会"。我们看人时，最好随时都有礼貌地正视着对方（make good eye contact）。而 keep eye contact 则是指"持续看对方的眼睛"，让对方知道你很专心，也表示尊重。

- I couldn't tell how she really felt, since she barely made **eye contact** through the entire interview.
  我看不出她到底感觉如何，因为面试时她几乎没有正眼看过我。

bring up 提出；提起

bring up 是指在谈话中提起某个话题或问题，通常可用动词 raise 代替。此外，bring up 还有"抚养"的意思。

- Don't ever **bring up** politics with Greg. He hates politics.
  别跟格里格提起政治。他讨厌政治。

听力小测验 GIVE IT A TRY!

Photograph

You will hear four statements about a picture. Choose the one statement that best describes what you see in the picture. The statements will be spoken only one time.

Ans: _____

Listening Comprehension

Listen to the conversation and answer the following questions.

1. a. ☐ Make good eye contact.
   b. ☐ Answer all questions politely.
   c. ☐ Dress in casual clothes.

2. a. ☐ Job requirements.
   b. ☐ Vacations.
   c. ☐ Working hours.

面试——
谈论自己

DURING AN INTERVIEW—
TALKING ABOUT ONESELF

面试时展示自己的**8**大要点

在面试时，应把握"展示自己"的机会，并注意下列几点：

❶ 尽量保持仪态端庄自然，说话有自信，但不要显得自大傲慢。

❷ 不要让不经意的肢体语言（body language）使人感觉自己笨拙而不自在（awkward and uncomfortable）。

❸ 一开始握手就要表现出热诚与积极。

❹ 说话语调要自信稳定，略带颤抖的声音，会让对方以为你紧张或缺乏信心。

❺ 强调你适合这份工作，包括性格与做事方法。

❻ 你的工作经验对公司很有帮助，可立刻进入工作状态。

❼ 你的职业生涯规划和这个职位很相称。

❽ 你最特别的地方——个人特质。

Josie is interviewing for a position at Sun Tech.
She is talking with the personnel manager,[1]
Mr. Jake Lancer.

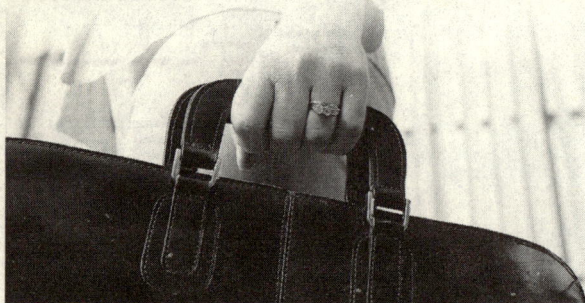

Jake: Tell me a little about yourself.

Josie: Originally,[2] I'm from Los Angeles.

Jake: What **brought** you **to the East Coast**?

Josie: I came to New York to attend school—
college. And I've come to love it so much
that I've decided to stay and find work.

Jake: What work experience do you have?

Josie: I worked as an intern[3] for a small
newspaper. And my primary responsibilities
were to sell newspaper advertisements to
businesses.

Jake: And what did that experience teach you?

Josie: I learned that I really enjoy sales, and I want to pursue⁴ a career in sales and marketing.

Jake: How would your former employer describe you?

Josie: He told me that my sales skills were an asset⁵ to the company. And he thanked me for my loyalty.

Jake: You seem very mature for your age. And I see from your résumé that you are very goal-**oriented**.

Josie: Thank you. I believe I've learned these things from my parents. They're my role models.⁶ However, I know I have a lot to learn.

---

1. personnel manager [ˌpɜsṇˋɛl ˋmænɪdʒɚ] 人事经理
2. originally [əˋrɪdʒənlɪ] *adv.* 起初地；原来地
3. intern [ˋɪntɜn] *n.* 实习生
4. pursue [pɚˋsu] *v.* 追求；追寻
5. asset [ˋæsɛt] *n.* 资产；有价值的事物
6. role model [ˋrol ˌmɑdḷ] 模范；榜样

中文翻译   TRANSLATION

乔西正在太阳科技公司面试。她正在和人事经理杰克·兰瑟先生面谈。

Jake: 告诉我一些关于你自己的事。

Josie: 我来自洛杉矶。

Jake: 你为什么会到东海岸来呢？

Josie: 我来纽约是为了读书——上大学。而我深深地爱上了纽约，所以决定留下来找工作。

Jake: 你有什么工作经验？

Josie: 我在一家小报社实习过，主要的工作职责是向商家推销报纸广告。

Jake: 你从那次经验中学到了什么？

Josie: 我发现我真的很喜欢做销售，并且想往销售和营销领域发展。

Jake: 你之前的老板会怎么形容你？

Josie: 他说我的销售技巧对公司很有帮助。而且他很感激我的忠诚。

Jake: 以你的年纪来说，你似乎相当成熟。而且从你的履历表看得出来，你很会做目标规划。

Josie: 谢谢你。我想这些都是从我爸妈那里学来的。他们是我的榜样。不过，我知道我还有很多东西要学习。

学习重点

---

bring (someone) to (somewhere)
带（某人）到（某地）去

字面上是说"把（某人）带到（某地）去"，常用 what brings you here（是什么风把你吹到这里）来询问对方到来的原因。

● It was the great weather that **brought** me **to** Florida for my retirement.

我是因为佛罗里达的天气很好，才来这里过退休生活。

---

the East Coast（美国）东海岸

美国幅员辽阔，提到一些小城市往往不是人尽皆知，因此常以比较大的区域来指称，例如：the East Coast（东海岸）、the West Coast（西海岸）、the Midwest（中西部）、the Northwest（西北部）、the South West（西南部）、the South（南部）。

● Debbie was born in **the Midwest**, but her family moved to **the East Coast** when she was five years old.

黛比出生于中西部，但是她家在她5岁时搬到了东海岸。

---

oriented 有……趋向性的

oriented 前面可接名词形成复合词，指"有……趋向性的；以……为导向的"，例如：export-oriented company（出口导向型的公司）、detail-oriented mind（讲究细节的思考模式）。

● Bill is a very fashion-**oriented** person. His outfits are always very trendy.

比尔是个很讲究时尚的人。他的衣服总是非常时髦。

GIVE IT A TRY!

Photograph

You will hear four statements about a picture. Choose the one statement that best describes what you see in the picture. The statements will be spoken only one time.

Ans: _____

Listening Comprehension

Listen to the conversation and answer the following questions.

1. *a.* ☐ Because she liked New York very much.

   b. ☐ Because her boyfriend was in New York.

   c. ☐ Because her family was in New York.

2. *a.* ☐ She worked for a trading company.

   b. ☐ She worked for a publishing company.

   c. ☐ She worked for a newspaper.

面试——
谈论工作细节

DURING AN INTERVIEW—
TALKING ABOUT THE JOB

网络搜寻相关职位

目前，随着电子商务（e-commerce）的风行，很多公司都开设了自己的网站，因此在面试前，不妨先上网了解一下这家公司的情况。此外，网页里也常有职位空缺（vacancy）的相关消息，可以借此事先了解工作性质、要求等，如此才能在面试时，充分掌握自己的优势和对方提出的条件。而面试时除了了解工作内容外，一般还会提及薪资、工作时间和休假，以及公司的福利政策，包括社保（social insurance）、医保（medical insurance）、在职培训（professional development／training）、退休制度（retirement plan）、股票认购权（stock option）等，有的还提供公司用车（company car）、差旅津贴（travel allowance）或住宿津贴（housing allowance）等福利。

此外，市面上常有招聘杂志或产业信息小册子，也可以从中获得一些相关信息，有的甚至还提供比较与分析，对掌握相关信息颇有帮助。

对话范例　　　　　　　　　　**DIALOGUE**

Here, Josie is interviewing for a job at Sun Tech. She is asking Jake some questions about the job.

Josie: Can you tell me a bit about the job responsibilities?

Jake: Of course. As salesman for our company, you would be required[1] to find new customers and **follow up on** our existing customers.[2]

Josie: Oh, so I would have the opportunity to generate my own sales **leads**.

Jake: Certainly. You would locate[3] prospective customers[4] and set up meetings with them to introduce our products.

Josie: And what are the **office hours**?

Jake: Our office hours are nine to five thirty, Monday through Friday. I bet you're curious about the salary for this position.

Josie: All right. I admit I am a little curious.

Jake: Well, the salary depends on experience, of course, but the **base salary** for sales is twenty-four thousand a year.

Josie: OK. And may I ask what benefits you offer?

Jake: We have paid holidays, a one-week paid vacation[5] in the first year, a retirement plan,[6] and bonuses if you meet sales targets.

Josie: That sounds reasonable.

---

1. require [rɪˋkwaɪr] v. 需要；必须
2. existing customer [ɪgˋzɪstɪŋ ˏkʌstəmə] 现有的客户
3. locate [ˋloket] v. 找到；锁定
4. prospective customer [prəˋspɛktɪv ˏkʌstəmə] 潜在客户
5. paid vacation [ˋped ˏvekeʃən] 带薪休假
6. retirement plan [rɪˋtaɪrmənt ˏplæn] 退休制度；退休计划

中文翻译

乔西现在在太阳科技面试。她正在询问杰克一些有关工作的问题。

Josie: 你能不能告诉我一些相关的工作内容?

Jake: 当然可以。要当我们公司的销售人员,你必须要能开发新客户,并且和老客户维持良好关系。

Josie: 哦,所以我有机会自己开发资源啦。

Jake: 那当然。你要锁定潜在的客户,和他们约时间介绍我们的产品。

Josie: 那么上班时间是怎样的?

Jake: 我们的上班时间是从周一到周五,每天九点到五点半。我敢说你一定对这份工作的薪水感到好奇吧。

Josie: 是的,我承认我是有一点好奇。

Jake: 嗯,薪水当然要视工作经验而定,不过销售人员的底薪是一年2.4万美元。

Josie: 好的。那我可不可以问一下你们提供什么样的福利?

Jake: 我们在国家法定假日薪水照付,第一年有7天年假,有退休制度,如果业绩达到标准还有红利。

Josie: 听起来挺合理的。

学习重点

. . . .

follow up on 采取进一步行动

与 follow (something) up 意思相同，都是表示"对（某事物）采取进一步行动"。用在客户身上当然是指"继续和客户联络，保持良好关系"。

● The police need to **follow up on** the tips they received about the bank robbery.

　　警方必须继续追踪关于这宗银行抢劫案的一些线索。

. . . .

lead 机会；线索

商业用语中，lead 常用来指"谈成生意、做成业务的机会"，所以 sales leads 有"商机"的意思。

● My calls today generated only one possible **lead**.

　　我今天所打的电话里只有一通有可能谈成生意的机会。

. . . .

office hours 上班时间

公司大部分都会规定员工的上班时间（office hours），而实际上的工作时长（working hours）通常都会比上班时间要多。

● **Office hours** end at five, but I'm often at my desk until seven.

　　我们公司五点下班，但我通常会待到七点。

. . . .

base salary 底薪

也可称作 base pay，其中 salary 与 pay 都表示"薪水；薪资"之意。和薪水相关的用语有 bonus（红利）、commission（佣金）、benefits（津贴）等。

● What is the average **base salary** for an engineer?

　　工程师的平均底薪是多少？

听力小测验

Listening Comprehension

Listen to the conversation and answer the following questions.

1. *a.* ☐ Eight to six.
   b. ☐ Nine to five.
   c. ☐ Nine to five thirty.

2. *a.* ☐ The company history.
   b. ☐ Promotions.
   c. ☐ The salary.

3. *a.* ☐ Thirty thousand a year.
   b. ☐ Twenty-four thousand a year.
   c. ☐ Forty thousand a year.

4. *a.* ☐ Meet sales targets.
   b. ☐ Write a report.
   c. ☐ Do a presentation.

上班第一天
FIRST DAY AT WORK

常见的公司组织部门

- Marketing 营销部
- Accounting 会计部
- Sales 销售部
- Personnel 人事部
- Human Resources 人力资源部
- Administration 行政部
- R & D (Research and Development) 研发部
- MIS (Management Information Systems) 信息管理部
- Production / Manufacturing 制造部；生产部
- Purchasing / Procurement 采购部
- Shipping / Delivery 货运（物流）部

Josie has been hired by Sun Tech as a sales representative. She has just arrived for her first day at work and is talking to her new coworker,[1] Rob Gardener.

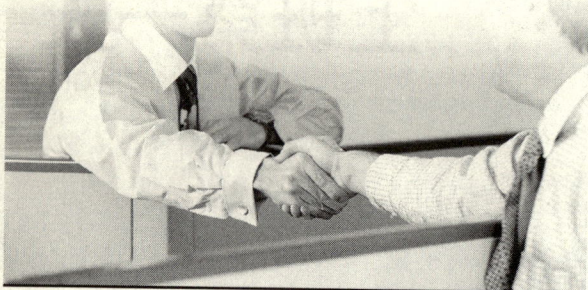

Rob: I'll give you a short tour of the office, show you your desk, and you can **get settled** in.

Josie: Thank you. I'd appreciate that.

Rob: The marketing department is right there. The accounting department is at the end of the hall.[2] This is the sales department, and the president's office is over there.

Josie: And my desk?

Rob: Your desk is right here next to mine.

Josie: But it looks like someone has already taken this desk.

Rob: Oh, that. No, that's a stack[3] of customer files[4] that I put on your desk, so you can start contacting[5] them right away and following up on their **orders**.

Josie: All right. Sounds good.

Rob: The rest rooms are around the corner; the watercooler[6] is right over there. Any questions so far?

Josie: Just one. When's lunch?

Rob: Lunch? Lunch is twelve to one. And if you have any other questions, please let me know. **Welcome aboard**, Josie.

Josie: Thanks, Rob.

---

1. coworker [koˋwɜkə] n. 同事
2. hall [hɔl] n. 门厅；走廊
3. stack [stæk] n. 一堆；一叠
4. file [faɪl] n. 档案
5. contact [ˋkɑntækt] v. 接洽；联系
6. watercooler [ˋwɑtəˌkulə] n. 饮水机

中文翻译

乔西被录取成为太阳科技的销售人员。她第一天到公司上班，正在和新同事罗伯·嘉登纳对话。

Rob: 我会带你简单参观一下办公室，告诉你位子在哪里，好让你一切就绪。

Josie: 谢谢你，我十分感激。

Rob: 营销部就在那边。走道尽头是会计部。销售部门在这里，总裁的办公室在那边。

Josie: 那我的位子在哪里？

Rob: 你的位子在这儿，就在我隔壁。

Josie: 但是看起来好像已经有人坐了。

Rob: 哦，那个啊。不是的，那叠是我放到你桌上的客户档案，以便使你可以马上开始和他们联络，并追踪他们的订单。

Josie: 好的。听起来还不错。

Rob: 洗手间在转角处；饮水机就在那边。到目前为止，有没有什么问题？

Josie: 只有一个。午休是什么时候？

Rob: 午休啊？午休是从十二点到一点。如果你还有任何问题，请告诉我。乔西，欢迎你加入。

Josie: 谢谢你，罗伯。

学习重点

get settled 准备就绪

搬到一个新的地方时常会用到这句话。settle 表示"安置；安顿"，get settled 则是"把一切安置妥当"，也就是"准备就绪"之意。

● It took me a month to **get settled** into my new apartment.

我花了一个月才把我新公寓安置妥当。

order 订单

order 原意是"命令；规则"，在商务英语中，则是"订单，汇票"的意思。例如：order form（订货单）、order book（订货簿）、money order（汇票）。

● The large **order** I placed with Digicom will arrive next week.

我向数码通信公司下了一笔大订单，货下周会到。

welcome aboard 欢迎加入

aboard 这个副词是指"在船、飞机、火车或公交车等交通工具上"。welcome aboard 原本是空中小姐对乘客的欢迎词，后来被引用到日常生活中，表示"欢迎加入"。

● Our new team member was **welcomed aboard** with a special dinner.

我们举办一个特别的晚宴来欢迎新组员的加入。

听力小测验

Photographs

You will hear four statements about a picture. Choose the one statement that best describes what you see in the picture. The statements will be spoken only one time.

Ans: _____

Ans: _____

Question and Response

You will hear a question or statement and three responses. Choose the best response to the question or statement. They will be spoken only one time.

1. _____ 2. _____ 3. _____ 4. _____

适应新工作
SETTLING INTO A NEW DESK

上班族的上班守则

一般朝九晚五（nine to five）的上班族，每天早上都要打卡上班（punch in），扣除中午的午休时间（lunch break），一天要工作8个小时，因此上班时间可不要表现出一副神情散漫（lounge）的样子；不过部分公司有规定的休息时段（coffee break），可以忙里偷闲一下。

有些嗜烟如命者忍不住烟瘾，非要每隔一段时间就吞云吐雾一番不可，那么记得要到吸烟区（smoking area）去，因为办公室都是禁烟的，甚至有些办公大楼为避免烟雾滞留于空调系统（AC）中而实施全面禁烟措施，因此要吸烟只好到户外去了！

如果要请病假（sick leave），得先打电话请假（call in sick）；至于出差（business trip），因为是基于公务的需要，可申请差旅费（travel allowance）；而下班时，也别忘了要先打卡下班（punch out），再带着你的公文包（briefcase）离开。

对话范例 / DIALOGUE

Josie is **settling into** her new desk at Sun Tech. Her coworker Rob is helping her out.

Rob: How do you like your new desk?

Josie: It's great. It looks like someone organized[1] it for me. They even arranged the files on my desk.

Rob: That was me. I know a first day on the job can be a bit overwhelming,[2] so I thought I'd help out a bit.

Josie: Thanks, Rob. Oh, if I run out of **supplies**,[3] where should I go to get some more?

Rob: There is a supply cupboard over there, next to the secretary's desk. If you need something, just let her know and you can **sign for** it.

Josie: OK. I think I'm ready to start calling these customers.

Rob: Wait. I haven't given you your new business cards.[4] Our office numbers[5] are on here, along with your extension number.[6]

Josie: Hey, these are nice. Thank you.

Rob: You're welcome. If you need anything else, just let me know. And don't forget to press nine when you **dial** on these phones. Good luck.

---

1. organize ['ɔrgə,naɪz] v. 整理；编排
2. overwhelming [,ovə'hwɛlmɪŋ, evo'] adj. 无法抗拒的；压倒性的
3. supply [sə'plaɪ] n. 消耗品；供应
4. business card ['bɪznɪs ,kɑrd] 名片
5. office number ['ɔfɪs ,nʌmbə] 办公室电话
6. extension number [ɪk'stɛnʃən ,nʌmbə] 分机号码

中文翻译

乔西正在适应她在太阳科技的新职位。她的同事罗伯在帮她。

Rob: 你觉得新办公桌怎么样？

Josie: 太棒了。看起来好像已经有人帮我整理过了。甚至连我桌上的档案夹都排好了。

Rob: 那是我排的。我知道第一天上班可能会有点忙不过来，所以我想我可以帮点忙。

Josie: 罗伯，谢谢你。哦，如果我的文具用品用完了，要到哪里去领取？

Rob: 秘书座位旁边有个储物柜。如果你需要什么，只要告诉她一声，然后签个名就可以拿了。

Josie: 好的。我想我已经准备好，可以开始打电话给客户了。

Rob: 等一下，我还没有把你的新名片给你。我们公司的电话以及你的分机号码都在上面。

Josie: 嘿，还挺不错的，谢谢。

Rob: 不客气。还有什么需要就告诉我一声。还有别忘记在拨打电话之前，要先按9。祝你好运。

学习重点

settle into 适应

类似的短语还有 get used to，用来表示"适应新的环境、工作等"。

● Since her coworkers were so friendly, it didn't take Amy long to **settle into** her office.

由于艾美的同事都很友善，她没多久就适应了办公室的环境。

supplies 耗用品；消耗品

这里的 supplies 指的是办公室的一些必需消耗品，如文具用品（stationery）、便利贴（Post-its）、碳粉（toner）和纸杯（paper cups）等。

● The bookstore down the street will have some of the **supplies** you're looking for.

街上的那家书店会有一些你要找的用品。

sign for (something) 签收（某物）

公司一般在收到东西或货品后，都会要求填写收据（receipt）、表格（form）或文件（document），表示确实收到过东西，将来可以作为凭证。

● You have to **sign for** this piece of mail.

你必须签收这封信。

dial 打电话

老式电话有拨号盘，因此用 dial（拨）来表示打电话。

● In order to **dial** out, you have to press zero on this phone.

要用这部电话拨外线，你必须先按0。

听力小测验

Photographs

You will hear four statements about a picture. Choose the one statement that best describes what you see in the picture. The statements will be spoken only one time.

Ans: _____

Ans: _____

Listening Comprehension

Listen to the conversation and answer the following questions.

a. ☐ Oh. b. ☐ Nine. c. ☐ Seven.

办公室
电脑的使用
COMPUTERS AT THE OFFICE

电脑的种类

在个人电脑（personal computer，简称为PC）越来越普及的今天，一些更轻薄小巧的电脑，如笔记本电脑（notebook computer，又称为laptop）或个人数码助理（personal digital assistant，简称为PDA，又称个人掌上电脑），也越来越风行。

其实，除了一般常见的IBM相容性个人电脑（IBM-compatible PC）之外，还有苹果公司（Apple）研发的麦金塔电脑（Macintosh，简称Mac）。使用一台电脑要先开机（boot up），一般IBM-compatible PC的操作系统（operating system，简称OS）以Windows居多，而电脑在执行（run）所有开机程序后，才能开始使用应用程序（application）。另外，使用后记得要关机（shut down）。

对话范例 DIALOGUE

As Josie gets off[1] the phone with her last customer, her coworker Rob comes over to **check up on** her.

Rob: So, how did it go?

Josie: Great! I contacted everyone and introduced myself, and I think I even got a new lead.

Rob: On your first day?! What **beginner's luck**!

Josie: Now, I just have to organize these names and phone numbers!

Rob: There should be some software[2] on your computer that will do that for you.

Josie: Fantastic![3] Let me try to find it . . .

Rob: You could also download[4] information from your computer onto a PDA, like mine.

Josie: What a neat gadget![5]

Rob: It's more than that. For instance, if I'm out **on the road** with a client, I can get Internet access[6] with this.

Josie: I need to consider getting one of these. Hey, what just happened to my computer?

Rob: Looks like it crashed.[7] You'll have to restart[8] it. I'll ask a technician[9] to look at it.

Josie: Thanks, Rob. You know, I know I sound like a **broken record**, but I really appreciate all your help.

Rob: Don't mention it.

---

1. get off [ˌgɛtˈɔf] 讲完（电话）；下车
2. software [ˈsɔftˌwɛr] n. 软件
3. fantastic [fænˈtæstɪk] adj. 极好的
4. download [ˈdaʊnˌlod] v. 下载
5. gadget [ˈgædʒɪt] n. 小工具；小机械装置
6. access [ˈæksɛs] n. 使用；（电脑的）存取
7. crash [kræʃ] v. 死机
8. restart [riˈstɑrt] v. 重新开机
9. technician [tɛkˈnɪʃən] n. 技术人员

在乔西和最后一个客户讲完电话时，她的同事罗伯过来看看她的情况。

Rob:　　情况如何？

Josie:　　很好！我联络了每位客户并向他们作自我介绍，我想我甚至找到了一个生意机会。

Rob:　　上班的第一天啊？！新人运气真是好！

Josie:　　现在，我只要把这些名字和电话号码都整理清楚就好了！

Rob:　　你的电脑里应该有软件可以帮你整理。

Josie:　　太好了！让我找找看……

Rob:　　你也可以把资料从你的电脑下载到掌上电脑上，就像我用的这种。

Josie:　　好炫的小机器！

Rob:　　它的功能可不只这样。举例来说，如果我和客户在外面谈生意，我还可以用它来上网。

Josie:　　我应该考虑买一台。嘿，我的电脑怎么了？

Rob:　　看来是死机了。你必须重新开机。我会请技术人员来看一下。

Josie:　　谢谢你，罗伯。我知道我就像唱片卡带一样一直重复这句话，但是我真的很感谢你一直帮我忙。

Rob:　　不客气。

学习重点

check (up) on 查看；检查

check up on 后面接人，表示"查看一下对方的情况如何"；如果其后接的是事物，则表示"核对；检查"。

● I need to **check up on** Ed and see how he's doing.

我得去看一下艾德，看看他最近怎么样。

beginner's luck 新人运气好

有时新人或对情况毫不了解的人，常会有莫名其妙的好运气。

● The first time Ron played golf, he got a hole-in-one! That's what I call **beginner's luck**.

罗恩第一次打高尔夫球就打了个一杆进洞！那就是我所说的新人运气好。

on the road 出外谈生意

on the road 的字面意思是"在路上"，事实上指的是"在外奔波"，所以在文中译作"出外谈生意"。

● I've been **on the road** visiting clients for two weeks now.

到现在我已经花了两个星期出外拜访客户谈生意。

broken record 像唱片卡带一样不断重复

record 指的是以前老式的黑胶唱片。这种唱片如果坏了，电唱机便会卡带而重复播放同一段音乐，所以 broken record 就引申表示"不断重复说同样的话"。

● Sara sounds like a **broken record** when she complains about work.

莎拉抱怨她的工作时就像唱片卡带一样喋喋不休。

听力小测验 　　　　　　　GIVE IT A TRY!

Photographs

You will hear four statements about a picture. Choose the one statement that best describes what you see in the picture. The statements will be spoken only one time.

Ans: ____

Ans: ____

Ans: ____

自我介绍
INTRODUCING YOURSELF

职场上的各种职称

- president 总裁
- CEO (chief executive officer) 首席执行官
- director 总监
- vice president 副总裁
- assistant director 副总监
- general manager 总经理
- CAO (chief administrative officer) 首席行政官
- consultant 顾问
- HR (human resources) manager 人事经理
- assistant manager 助理、副经理
- supervisor 主任、督导
- specialist 专员
- secretary 秘书
- engineer 工程师
- technician 技师

Here, Josie introduces herself to a new coworker, Sally Jenkins.

Josie: Hi. **Allow** me **to** introduce myself. I'm Josie Gleason. I'm new here. I work in **Sales**.

Sally: Nice to meet you, Josie. My name is Sally Jenkins. I'm in the marketing department.[1] How long have you been here for?

Josie: Not very long. Only a few days. I started on Monday.

Sally: And how do you like it so far?

Josie: So far, it's been great. I like the job, and the people are very friendly and helpful.[2] How long have you been working here?

Sally: Six years, and I **can't complain**.

Josie: That's quite a while. You must really like it here.

Sally: I do, and you will, too. Listen, it was nice meeting you. I've got to get back to work.[3] Here's my card.

Josie: Great. We should **do lunch** sometime.

Sally: That would be great. Give me a call?

Josie: Maybe sometime next week?

Sally: Perfect. I look forward to[4] hearing from you.

Josie: Bye-bye.

Sally: OK. Bye.

---

1. department [dɪˈpɑrtmənt] *n.* 部门；单位
2. helpful [ˈhɛlpfəl] *adj.* 有帮助的
3. get back to work [ˌɡɛtˈbæk tə ˈwɜk] 回去工作
4. look forward to [ˈlʊk ˈfɔrwəd tu] 盼望；期待

中文翻译

现在，乔西正在向新同事莎莉·简金斯作自我介绍。

Josie: 嗨，容我自我介绍一下。我叫乔西·格利森。我是新来的，在销售部工作。

Sally: 很高兴认识你，乔西。我的名字叫莎莉·简金斯。我在营销部工作。你来公司多久了？

Josie: 没多久，才刚来几天。我星期一才开始上班的。

Sally: 那到目前为止你觉得怎么样？

Josie: 到目前为止，一切都很好。我喜欢这份工作，而且每个人都很友善、很热心。你在这里工作多久了？

Sally: 6年了，我没什么好挑剔的。

Josie: 那是挺久的。你一定是真的很喜欢这里的工作。

Sally: 是啊，你也会喜欢这里的。好了，很高兴认识你。我得回去工作了。这是我的名片。

Josie: 太好了。改天我们应该一起吃个午餐。

Sally: 那不错啊。打电话给我吧？

Josie: 下个星期约个时间如何？

Sally: 好啊，我等你的电话。

Josie: 再见。

Sally: 好的，再见。

学习重点

allow (someone) to V. 允许（某人）去……

allow是"准许；允许"的意思，而allow me to是英语里相当客气的用法，表示"容我……；允许我……"。

● **Allow** me **to** help you with your bags.

让我来帮你拿袋子。

Sales 销售部

口语中，可将department（部门）省去，只说部门名称即可。通常大小写皆可，不过为了避免误解，还是大写的形式出现得比较多。

● She's in **Marketing** and I'm in **Sales**.

她在营销部工作，而我在销售部。

can't complain 没什么好抱怨的

这是用来指事情或情况整体而言已经算不错了，即使有一些问题存在，但也没什么好抱怨的。

● A: How's your vacation going?

你假期过得如何？

● B: I **can't complain**. The weather here is great!

没什么好抱怨的。这里的天气真是好！

do lunch 吃午饭

这是相当口语的用法，办公室同事常一起吃午餐、晚餐或喝咖啡（do lunch / dinner / coffee）。也可用在娱乐或旅行方面，如do a movie（去看电影）、do the town（去城里玩）等。

● Next summer, when we both have a month's vacation, let's **do Europe**.

等明年夏天我俩都有一个月的假的时候，就一起去欧洲玩吧。

听力小测验   GIVE IT A TRY!

Photographs

You will hear four statements about a picture. Choose the
one statement that best describes what you see in the
picture. The statements will be spoken only one time.

Ans: _____

Ans: _____

Question and Response

You will hear a question or statement and three responses.
Choose the best response to the question or statement.
They will be spoken only one time.

1. _____   2. _____   3. _____   4. _____

工作上轨道

BECOMING FAMILIAR WITH OFFICE PROCEDURES

通信媒介

- note 便笺纸
- memo (memorandum) 备忘录
- telephone 电话
- video conference 视频会议
- fax (facsimile) 传真
- e-mail (electronic mail) 电子邮件
- voice mail 语音邮件
- video mail 影音邮件
- Intranet 组织内部的数码通信网络
- LAN (local area network) 局域网络
- WAN (wide area network) 广域网络
- Internet 因特网

对话范例   DIALOGUE

Josie asks her coworker Rob for some help with a few things in the office.

Josie: Rob. Do you have a minute to go over[1] these forms with me?

Rob: Of course. By the way, **buzz** around the office is that you're giving some of the **old-timers** in Sales some fresh competition.[2]

Josie: Really?

Rob: Yeah, and the manager is very pleased with how well you're doing.

Josie: I'm sure the people in Shipping have a completely different view.[3]

Rob: Probably.

Josie: Well, sales may **come easy** for me, but doing paperwork[4] definitely does not.

Rob: Don't worry. You'll **get the hang of** it. Most companies use similar forms.

Josie: So, you mean, I only need to learn one form?

Rob: Pretty much. They look different, but the content is pretty much the same.

Josie: That's a relief.[5] Hey, Rob. Would you mind teaching me how to use this voice mail system as well? Sorry for all the trouble, Rob.

Rob: No, no problem. Listen, once you learn the ropes, it'll become second nature to you.

---

1. go over [`go ˌovə] 仔细检查或察看
2. competition [ˌkɑmpə`tɪʃən] n. 竞争
3. view [vju] n. 观点；看法
4. paperwork [`pepəˌwɜk] n. 文书工作
5. relief [rɪ`lif] n. (痛苦、负担等的) 减轻；解除

中文翻译   TRANSLATION

乔西在办公室有些问题请她同事罗伯帮忙。

Josie:	罗伯,你有空跟我核对一下这些表格吗?
Rob:	当然了。对了,办公室有传言,你为暮气沉沉的销售部注入了一股活力。
Josie:	真的吗?
Rob:	是啊,而且经理对你的工作相当满意。
Josie:	我确定货运部的人看法可就完全不一样了。
Rob:	或许吧。
Josie:	嗯,销售对我来说可能易如反掌,但是文书工作可就不简单了。
Rob:	别担心,你会掌握诀窍的。大部分的公司使用的表格都很相似。
Josie:	所以,你的意思是我只要学会一种就好了吗?
Rob:	可以这么说。它们看起来虽然不一样,但是内容却是差不多的。
Josie:	那我就放心了。嘿,罗伯,你可不可以顺便教我怎么使用语音信箱系统?罗伯,抱歉给你添了这么多麻烦。
Rob:	不会,别客气。听好,一旦你掌握诀窍,就会习惯成自然了。

学习重点

buzz 传闻

原指蜜蜂的嗡嗡声，口语上引申为"闲言碎语"的意思。

- Hey, what's the **buzz** around the office these days?

  嘿，办公室最近又有什么传言？

old-timer 老手；老前辈

在口语中，old-timer是指久居一地或久任一职的人，也可以说 veteran（老手）。

- Jack is one of the **old-timers** in his department.

  杰克是该部门的老前辈之一。

come easy 轻而易举；很容易做到

easy本来是形容词，但在此作副词用，是口语用法，当然也可以用easily来替换。

- Everything **comes easy** for him, but the rest of us have to work really hard.

  他做任何事都是不费吹灰之力就能达成，而我们其他人就得苦干实干。

get the hang of (something) 掌握（某事）的诀窍

这是口语的用法。表示"了解（某事物）的意义；熟悉如何使用（某物）"。类似的说法还有learn the ropes，其中ropes是指某行业的情况、规则、手续等。而指导别人令其掌握诀窍则可说成 show (someone) the ropes。

- Using a computer is easy once you **get the hang of** it.

  一旦掌握窍门，使用电脑其实很简单。

听力小测验　　　　　　　　　　　　　GIVE IT A TRY!

Photographs

You will hear four statements about a picture. Choose the one statement that best describes what you see in the picture. The statements will be spoken only one time.

Ans: _____

Ans: _____

Ans: _____

接听电话
ANSWERING THE PHONE

电话分类与通话方式

一般的电话机有下列几种：

- car phone 车载电话
- cell phone, mobile phone 移动电话
- cordless phone 无线电话
- rotary phone 转盘式电话
- wall phone 壁挂式电话
- public phone 公共电话

通话方式可分为：

- credit card call 信用卡付费电话
- local call 市内电话
- long-distance call 长途电话
- collect call 对方付费电话
- Internet call 网络电话

对话范例　　　　　　　　　　　DIALOGUE

Sally Jenkins is the department secretary[1] in Sun Tech's marketing department. Here, she is answering a phone call.

Sally: Hello, this is Sally at Sun Tech. How may I **direct** your call?

Caller: Hi, Sally. Would you please transfer[2] me to Sam Palmer in Marketing, extension 334?

Sally: Whom may I say is calling?

Caller: This is Arthur Smith from Cell Phones Limited.

Sally: Please hold, Mr. Smith. I'll check to see if Mr. Palmer is **available** to **take** your **call**.

(A moment later . . .)

Sally: I'm sorry, Mr. Smith. Mr. Palmer's on another line. Would you care to **hold**, or would you like to leave a message[3] on his voice mail?[4]

Caller: I'll hold, but I'm calling long-distance.[5]

Sally: Oh! Well, in that case, I'll ask Mr. Palmer to call you back as soon as possible.

Caller: No, I can wait a few more minutes.

Sally: Oh, you're in luck! Mr. Palmer's line is free now. I'll transfer your call. Thanks for holding.

Caller: Thank you.

---

1. secretary [ˈsɛkrəˌtɛrɪ] *n.* 秘书
2. transfer [trænsˈfɝ] *v.* 转换；转到……
3. leave a message [ˈliv ə ˈmɛsɪdʒ] 留言
4. voice mail [ˈvɔɪs ˌmel] 语音信箱
5. long-distance [ˈlɔŋˈdɪstəns] *adv.* 长途电话

中文翻译   TRANSLATION

莎莉·简金斯是太阳科技营销部的秘书。她现在正在接听一通
电话。

Sally:　　您好，我是太阳科技的莎莉。请问您找哪位？

Caller:　　嗨，莎莉。麻烦请帮我转拨分机334，找营销部的山
　　　　　姆·帕姆尔好吗？

Sally:　　请问你是哪里？

Caller:　　我是赛尔电话有限公司的亚瑟·史密斯。

Sally:　　史密斯先生，请稍候。我看看帕姆尔先生现在能不能
　　　　　接您的电话。

　　　　　(不久……)

Sally:　　史密斯先生，很抱歉，帕姆尔先生正在另一条线上
　　　　　通话。您要稍等一下，还是要在他的语音信箱里留
　　　　　言？

Caller:　　我会等他，不过我这是长途电话。

Sally:　　哦！嗯，如果是这样的话，我会请帕姆尔先生尽快回
　　　　　电话给您。

Caller:　　不用，我可以再等几分钟。

Sally:　　哦，您运气真好！帕姆尔先生已经接完电话了，我帮
　　　　　您转接过去。谢谢您的等候。

Caller:　　谢谢你。

direct 转接到……

direct 可表示"指出方向"。电话用语中，direct a call 表示"将电话转接到某一分机"。

● The operator accidentally **directed** my call to the president's office.

总机不小心把我的电话接到总裁办公室。

available 有空的；能够的

available 在此是用来表示"某人有空或许可以做某事"，意思与 free 差不多。

● Are you **available** this Sunday?

你这个星期天有空吗？

take (someone's) call 接（某人打来的）电话

与 answer (someone's) call 同义，表示"接电话"，而 make a call 则是指"打电话"。

● I'm sorry I couldn't **take** your **call** earlier. I was with a client.

很抱歉我先前不能接你的电话。我刚刚跟客户在一起。

hold 稍候

在电话中常用 hold 来请对方稍等，不要挂断，其他类似的常用说法有 hold a second / moment, please 或 just a moment，意思都是"请稍候"。

● Can you **hold** a minute? I have another call on the other line.

你能不能稍等一下？我还有另外一个电话要接。

GIVE IT A TRY!

Listening Comprehension

Listen to the conversation and answer the following
questions.

1. *a.* ☐ Arthur Smith.
   b. ☐ Sam Palmer.
   c. ☐ Sally Jenkins.

2. *a.* ☐ Arthur Smith.
   b. ☐ Sam Palmer.
   c. ☐ Sally Jenkins.

3. *a.* ☐ Arthur Smith.
   b. ☐ Sam Palmer.
   c. ☐ Sally Jekins.

4. *a.* ☐ 344.
   b. ☐ 334.
   c. ☐ 433.

电话留言
LEAVING A MESSAGE

Code 复合词

英文中 code 这个词可以因使用语境的不同，而有不同的意义。code 可以表示"记号；符号"，例如：area code（电话区号）、zip code（邮政编码）、telegraph code（电报密码）。另外，code 也可以表示"规则；准则"的意思，例如：dress code（着装规定）、traffic code（交通规则）。在法律上，code 可与 bill 这个词相对，bill 指的是"尚未通过而仍在审议的提案或草案"，而 code 是已明文规定的"法典，法规"，例如 civil code（民法）、criminal code（刑法）等。

在计算机方面，code 一般是用来表示"指令"，也就是以特殊语言编写，并可通过转译成为计算机所能辨识的语言。在遗传学上，code 指的则是基因的排序，也就是所谓的 genetic code（遗传密码）。

对话范例 — DIALOGUE

Here, Sally answers another phone call, this one from Bill Willis.

Sally: Good Morning, Sun Tech. May I help you?

Caller: This is Mr. Willis of Connections Limited. I'm calling from Australia. May I speak to Sam Palmer in Marketing?

Sally: I'm sorry. Mr. Palmer is out of the office. May I take a message?

Caller: Do you expect[1] him back later today?

Sally: I'm afraid he'll be **out of town** all day.

Caller: **In that case**, you can leave a message. Please tell him that I'd like to talk to him **as soon as possible** about the new product design.[2]

Sally: OK. Is there any particular time that you want him to call you?

Caller: He can reach[3] me at my office any time tomorrow. My number is country code[4] 61, area code[5] 3, number 2775-2940.

Sally: OK. Let me repeat that back to you. Mr. Willis of Connections Limited, number 613-2775-2940; call back as soon as possible regarding the new product design. You can be reached all day tomorrow at that number.

Caller: That's correct.

Sally: OK, I'll give him the message, Mr. Willis, and he'll get back to you as soon as he can.

Caller: Thank you. Good-bye.

---

1. expect [ɪkˈspɛkt] v. 预计；预料
2. product design [ˈprɑdəkt dɪˈzaɪn] 产品设计
3. reach [ritʃ] v. 与（某人）取得联系
4. country code [ˈkʌntrɪ ˌkod] 国家编码
5. area code [ˈɛrɪə ˌkod] 区域编号

中文翻译

现在，莎莉接听另一通电话，是比尔·威利斯打来的。

Sally: 早上好，这里是太阳科技。有什么可以为您效劳的吗？

Caller: 我是联合有限公司的威利斯。我是从澳大利亚打来的。请帮我接营销部的山姆·帕姆尔好吗？

Sally: 抱歉，帕姆尔先生不在办公室。我可以帮您留个口信吗？

Caller: 你认为他今天晚一点会回来吗？

Sally: 恐怕他一整天都不会在。

Caller: 这样的话，我还是留言好了。请告诉他我想尽快和他讨论有关新产品设计的问题。

Sally: 好的，您要他在特定的时间打给您吗？

Caller: 明天任何时间他都可以打电话到我办公室找我。我的电话是国家编码61，区域编号3，电话号码2775-2940。

Sally: 好的，我重复一遍给您听。联合有限公司的威利斯先生，电话是613-2775-2940，请速回电，有关新产品设计的事，明天任何时间都可以打这个电话。

Caller: 没错。

Sally: 好的，威利斯先生，我会转告他，他会尽快回电给您的。

Caller: 谢谢你。再见。

out of town 出远门

town 表示"城市；城镇"，口语上说 out of town 就是"出远门；不在城里"的意思，反义词是 in town（在城里）。

● The Johnsons will be **out of town** for a few days, so I agreed to pick up their mail for them.

约翰逊一家人要出城几天，所以我同意帮他们收信。

in that case 若是那样的话

相关用语还有 in any case（无论如何）和 in no case（绝不）。

● A: I've heard that the Golden Theater's admission price is eight U.S. dollars.

我听说黄金戏院的门票是8美元。

B: **In that case**, let's just rent a movie from the video store.

那样的话，我们去录影带店租一部电影来看好了。

as soon as possible 尽快

此用语常以首字母缩略词 ASAP 表示。由于此用语有些不太礼貌，如果情况并不是真的很紧急，还是少用为妙。

● In reviewing your application, I noticed we are missing a list of references. Please forward it to us **ASAP**.

在看你的应聘资料时，我发现少了推荐名单，请尽快补上。

听力小测验   GIVE IT A TRY!

Listening Comprehension

Listen to the conversation and answer the following questions.

1.   *a.* ☐ America.
    b. ☐ Australia.
    c. ☐ Austria.

2.   *a.* ☐ No, he is not.
    b. ☐ Yes, he is.
    c. ☐ Maybe.

3.   *a.* ☐ The new product name.
    b. ☐ The new product price.
    c. ☐ The new product design.

4.   *a.* ☐ 16.
    b. ☐ 61.
    c. ☐ 51.

打国际电话
MAKING AN INTERNATIONAL CALL

打电话

英语中，telephone 本身可作动词或名词使用，因此打电话给别人可以说 telephone (someone)，也可以说成 call (someone)、give (someone) a call、ring (someone) up。要打电话给客户时，可以先到电话簿 (directory, phone book) 上找到对方的电话号码 (phone number)，然后再拨号 (dial)。如果你要找公司或商店的电话，则可以从黄页分类电话簿 (yellow pages) 中去找。

如果是拨对方付费电话 (collect call)，可以请接线员 (operator) 替你拨通，由对方来付费；若是直接拨打 (direct call)，其费用则需自行负担。而通过电脑拨打电话，则比较省事，只要输入电话号码，电脑就会帮你拨打至接通为止，不需要担心对方是否占线，但不易接通。其采用的方式也随科技的发展日新月异，有通过软件拨打与接收、通过硬件拨打与接收，以及通过硬件转换，经网络拨通对方电脑或家用电话等方式。也许随着宽频网络 (broadband) 的拓展，以后的电话会既方便又便宜。

对话范例 DIALOGUE

Sam Palmer is returning Bill Willis's call. He needs help from a telephone operator[1] as he makes an international[2] call.

Operator: Operator Assistance.[3] How may I help you?

Sam: Hi! I've been trying to make a direct call to Sydney, Australia, but there seems to be a problem with the line. I can't **get through**.

Operator: If you give me the number, I'll connect[4] you.

Sam: Certainly. The country code is 61, the area code is 3, and the number is 2775-2940. This is a business number.

Operator: All right. Please hold.

(A minute later . . .)

Operator: Sir, the line is open now, so I'll put you through.

Sam: Thanks, operator.

Bill: Mr. Willis speaking.

Sam: Hello, Mr. Willis. This is Sam Palmer, calling from Sun Tech. I'm sorry I missed your call yesterday.

Bill: Yeah. Thanks for getting back to me so promptly.[5] I have a couple of requests[6] **in regard to** product design.

Sam: I'm **all ears**. **Go ahead**, Mr. Willis.

Bill: Thanks. First of all . . .

---

1. operator [ˈɑpəˌretə] *n.* 接线员
2. international [ˌɪntəˈnæʃənl] *adj.* 国际的
3. assistance [əˈsɪstəns] *n.* 援助；帮忙
4. connect [kəˈnɛkt] *v.* 连接；联系
5. promptly [ˈprɑmptlɪ] *adv.* 迅速地
6. request [rɪˈkwɛst] *n.* 要求；请求

中文翻译   TRANSLATION

山姆·帕姆尔回电给比尔·威利斯。他请电话接线员帮他打国际
电话。

Operator: 接线服务，有什么可以效劳的吗？

Sam: 嗨！我一直试着要直接拨电话到澳大利亚悉尼，但是
线路好像有问题。我打不通。

Operator: 请您告诉我电话号码，我会帮您接通。

Sam: 当然可以。国家编码是61，区域编号3，电话号码是
2775-2940。这是公司电话。

Operator: 好的。请稍候。

（一分钟后……）

Operator: 先生，这条线现在没问题，我会帮您接通。

Sam: 谢谢你，接线员。

Bill: 喂，我是威利斯。

Sam: 喂，威利斯先生。我是太阳科技的山姆·帕姆尔。很
抱歉昨天没有接到您的电话。

Bill: 哦，谢谢您这么快就回电话给我。关于产品的设计，
我有几个要求。

Sam: 我洗耳恭听。请继续说，威利斯先生。

Bill: 谢谢。首先……

学习重点

get through (电话)接通；联络

此短语有许多不同的用法，如 get through an examination（通过考试）、get through with work（完成工作），但在电话用语中，get through 指"联系到；接通电话"。

- I can't **get through** to Paris.

  我联系不到巴黎的人。

in regard to 关于

也可以说成 in relation to，表示"关于……"的意思，也可用 with regard to 或 regarding 代替。

- **In regard to** our meeting, it will be held in the conference room.

  关于我们的会议，将会在会议室举行。

all ears 洗耳恭听

从字面上"所有的耳朵都在听"可知这句话的意思是"洗耳恭听"，类似的用语 all eyes 则是指"全神贯注"。而最怕的是 go in one ear and out the other（一耳进一耳出），把别人说的话当耳边风，早晚会出纰漏的。

- Joe was **all ears** when I mentioned Ian's name.

  当我提到伊恩的名字时，乔便全神贯注地倾听。

go ahead 继续

这是个常用的短语，用来请别人继续说或做所提到的事。

- I have work to do, so **go ahead** without me.

  我有工作要做，所以你有事就先去做不用管我。

听力小测验　　　　　　　　　GIVE IT A TRY!

Listening Comprehension

Listen to the conversation and answer the following questions.

1. a. ☐ He couldn't get through.
   b. ☐ He spent too much money to make the call.
   c. ☐ He had the wrong number.

2. a. ☐ Nobody.
   b. ☐ The the operator.
   c. ☐ Sam's friend.

3. a. ☐ 2775-2904.
   b. ☐ 2775-2940.
   c. ☐ 2775-2490.

4. a. ☐ Yes, he is.
   b. ☐ No, he is not.
   c. ☐ We don't know.

查看电子邮件
CHECKING E-MAIL

计算机病毒

就像身体会受到病毒（virus）感染一样，电脑也有所谓的"病毒"。电脑病毒是一种会妨碍电脑正常运行的程序，电脑中毒以后，储存在硬盘（hard disk）里的资料（data）或信息（information）都有可能会被感染，一传十，十传百，一下子就都塞满了垃圾箱（garbage）；更厉害的病毒还可能使硬盘里的资料全部被删除（wiped out）或者把硬盘格式化（formatted），造成原有资料全部遗失。

通常计算机病毒是由网络下载（download）伴随而来的，或是使用过含有病毒的软盘（floppy disk），导致病毒入侵系统。虽然现在有很多防毒软件（antivirus software），但是计算机病毒还是每天在网络上流窜着，尤其采用 ADSL 或 cable modem 全天连线的家用电脑，常成为黑客（hacker）下手的目标，因而更要提高警觉。所以预防电脑中毒最好的方法，就是不要随便在网站上下载，并注意来路不明的 e-mail，随时启动病毒监测程序（virus-checking program），甚至设置个人防火墙（firewall）来预防。

对话范例

Mary Jordan, an assistant sales manager[1] in the sales department, has returned to the office from a two-week vacation. Her coworker, David Franks, welcomes her back.

Mary: Hi, David. Did anyone miss me?

David: Of course. I even have the messages to prove it. Here's an urgent[2] one from Dale.

Mary: Is there a problem?

David: I'm not sure. He e-mailed you last week and was calling to see if you were back in town.

Mary: I guess I'd better check my e-mail first thing.

David: Here's a list of people who called. I don't think any of them are urgent.

Mary: Thanks, David. It's nice to know there's someone to **hold down the fort**. I'm going to check my e-mail right now. Yikes! There are forty-five messages in my inbox!

David: I'll bet a lot of them are junk mail.[3]

Mary: I can only hope! It's amazing how fast this stuff **stacks up**.

David: Oh, if you see any addresses that look questionable, check this list. There are some new viruses[4] circulating.[5]

Mary: Thanks. **The last thing** we need is an entire system shutdown[6] because of a computer virus.

David: **You can say that again**.

---

1. assistant sales manager [əˈsɪstənt ˌselz ˈmænɪdʒə] 业务助理；销售助理
2. urgent [ˈɜdʒənt] *adj.* 紧急的
3. junk mail [ˈdʒʌŋk ˌmel] 垃圾邮件
4. virus [ˈvaɪrəs] *n.* 病毒
5. circulate [ˈsɜkjəˌlet] *v.* 流传；传播
6. shutdown [ˈʃʌtˌdaʊn] *n.* 关闭；关掉

中文翻译 TRANSLATION

玛丽·乔丹是销售部的助理,她休假两个星期之后刚刚回到公司。她的同事大卫·弗兰克斯欢迎她回来。

Mary: 嗨,大卫。有没有人想念我啊?

David: 当然有了,我甚至有一些留言可证明。这里有条戴尔给你的紧急留言。

Mary: 是不是有什么问题?

David: 我不太确定。他上周发了电子邮件给你,还打电话来问你回来了没。

Mary: 我想我最好先查查我的电子邮箱。

David: 这里是来电者名单。我想这些都不是紧急事件。

Mary: 谢了,大卫。知道有人帮我处理一些事务真是不错。我现在要看看我的电子邮件了。天哪!我的收件箱里有45封信!

David: 我敢说一定有很多是垃圾邮件。

Mary: 但愿如此!这些信件累积的速度真惊人。

David: 哦,如果你看到什么可疑的地址,先看一下这张清单。有一些新病毒正在传播。

Mary: 谢了。我们最不希望的就是因为计算机病毒而让整个系统都坏掉。

David: 你说得一点也没错。

学习重点

. . . .

hold down the fort 暂时代理别人的工作

fort是"堡垒"，hold down the fort字面上是"守住堡垒"，引申表示"某人不在时，暂时替他处理一些事务"。

● When her mother is away, Jane has to **hold down the fort**.

妈妈不在家时，简就得代理持家。

. . . .

stack up 堆积

stack up或pile up可用来形容具体文件的堆积，或是抽象地形容未完成的工作"越堆越多"。

● I should never have let these files **stack up** like this!

我真不该让文件堆成这样！

. . . .

the last thing 最不希望发生的事

the last原指"最后的；最晚的"，在此用来指"最不可能的；最不愿意的"，所以the last thing就是指"最不愿意发生的事；最不可能做的事"。

● It was **the last thing** I expect him to do.

我认为那是他最不可能做的事。

. . . .

you can say that again 你说得很对

这是口语中常用的一句话，字面意思是"你可以再说一遍"，实际上是表示非常赞同对方说的话，也就是指"你说得对"，类似的说法还有you said it。

● A: It sure is cold today.

今天真的好冷。

B: Yeah, **you can say that again**.

是啊，你说得很对。

GIVE IT A TRY!

Listening Comprehension

Listen to the conversation and answer the following questions.

1. *a.* ☐ An urgent task.

   b. ☐ A list of phone calls.

   c. ☐ A model of fort.

2. *a.* ☐ Check her e-mail.

   b. ☐ Stack up her books.

   c. ☐ Look in her address book.

3. *a.* ☐ 45.

   b. ☐ 40.

   c. ☐ 35.

4. *a.* ☐ A computer virus shutting down the system.

   b. ☐ A vacation that lasts the entine winter.

   c. ☐ An effective system to check the woman's e-mail.

投资股市

INVESTING IN THE STOCK MARKET

股票的相关用语

股票是一种有价证券。公司经营需要大量资金（funds／capital），可召开公开说明会，向社会大众募集资金。在集资时，发给投资人一张有价证券，载明所拥有的股份，就称为股票（shares／stock）。而持有股票者就是该公司的股东（shareholder／stockholder）。第一次公开发行的股票，称为IPO（initial public offering）。下面再列出一些相关用语：

- long-term investment [ˈlɔŋˌtəm ɪnˈvɛstmənt]
  长期投资
- day trader [ˈdeˌtredə] 天天玩股票的人
- bond [bɑnd] 债券；公债
- security [sɪˈkjʊrətɪ] 有价证券
- skyrocket [ˈskaɪˌrɑkɪt] 飙升
- crash [kræʃ] 崩盘；猛跌
- listed [ˈlɪstɪd] 上市的

Paul Cramer is having lunch with his coworker, Jake Lancer, and Jake is asking him for advice.

Jake: I've been thinking about getting into the stock market,[1] but I don't know where to start. What do you know about buying stocks?

Paul: Well, I have a few investments.[2] Come to think of it, now is probably a good time to invest. The market is low, so prices are probably pretty good.

Jake: Well, what kind of stock do you suggest?

Paul: If you want to make money quickly, you could try speculating.[3]

Jake: What do you mean by speculating?

Paul: You buy stocks that go up quickly and then sell quickly for a fast profit. But it's risky.[4] Stocks that go up fast also tend to go down fast.

Jake: Yeah, I see what you mean.

Paul: You just have to guess how high they'll go, and then sell when you think they're about to come down. But you could **lose your shorts** if you guess wrong.

Jake: Hmm, I'm **not much of a** gambler.[5]

Paul: So you probably want to stick to[6] **blue-chip stocks** for a guaranteed return on your investment.

Jake: That sounds right up my alley.

---

1. stock market [`stɑk ˌmɑrkɪt] 股市
2. investment [ɪn`vɛstmənt] 投资
3. speculate [`spɛkjəˌlet] v. （股市、土地等）投机
4. risky [`rɪskɪ] adj. 有风险的；冒险的
5. gambler [`gæmblə] n. 赌徒
6. stick to [`stɪk `tu] 锁定；坚持；固守

保罗·克莱默正在和他同事杰克·兰瑟吃午餐，杰克在问他的意见。

Jake: 我一直想进股票市场，但是不知道从哪里开始。你对买股票了解多少？

Paul: 嗯，我自己投资了一些。想到这，现在可能是投资的好时机。现在股市正低迷，所以价位应该相当不错。

Jake: 那么，你建议买什么股票？

Paul: 如果你想快速致富，你可以试着投机一下。

Jake: 你所谓的投机是什么意思？

Paul: 你买会飙升的股票，然后尽快脱手，快速获利。但是这样有风险。涨得快的股票往往跌得也快。

Jake: 是啊，我懂你的意思。

Paul: 你必须先预测会涨多少，然后在你认为快要下跌的时候卖掉。但是如果你猜错了，有可能会赔得很惨。

Jake: 嗯，我这个人不太会投机。

Paul: 那么你最好锁定绩优股，投资回报比较有保障。

Jake: 听起来正适合我。

学习重点

lose your shorts 输光；赔光

也可以说成 lose your shirts。shorts 是指"短裤"，连身上的短裤、衬衫都赔光了，所以表示"赔得很惨"。

● I'm not going to risk **losing my shorts** just to help a relative gamble in penny stocks.

我才不会只为了帮一个亲戚玩低价股而冒让自己输光的风险。

not much of a (something) 不擅长（某事物）

此语是用来表达某人"不擅长（某事物）"，例如：not much of a dancer / swimmer / player（舞跳得不好 / 不太会游泳 / 球打得不好）。

● I'm **not much of a** drinker. I don't really care for alcohol.

我不太会喝酒。我不是很喜欢酒。

blue-chip stock 蓝筹股；绩优股

也可直接用名词 blue chip 来代替。blue chip 原本是指赌桌上蓝色的高价值筹码，引申为"绩优股"。加了连字符的 blue-chip 可以当形容词用，表示"绩优的；杰出的"。

● For a safe investment, buy **blue-chip stocks**.

想要稳当的投资，就要买绩优股。

听力小测验　　　　　　　　　　　　**GIVE IT A TRY!**

Listening Comprehension

Listen to the conversation and answer the following questions.

1. *a.* ☐ Yes, it is.

   b. ☐ No, it is not.

   c. ☐ We don't know.

2. *a.* ☐ Getting a new job.

   b. ☐ Getting into the stock market.

   c. ☐ Getting a raise.

3. *a.* ☐ He should buy stocks that go up fast.

   b. ☐ He should try to avoid all risky stocks.

   c. ☐ He should stop speculating on the market.

4. *a.* ☐ continue to climb.

   b. ☐ are impossible to sell.

   c. ☐ drop in value later.

股市涨跌
STOCK MARKET FLUCTUATIONS

股市里的涨跌停板

有些证券交易所规定，股价升降幅度超过前一交易日收盘价格的10%，将停止升降 (rise or drop)，因此这个上下10%的限度就称为涨停板或跌停板；但有些则没有这样的规定。如果股票行情看涨 (uptrend)，就称为"牛市" (bull market) 或"多头市场"；反之，若股价一路下滑 (downtrend)，就称为"熊市" (bear market) 或"空头市场"。以牛和熊来比喻股市行情，可能是来自于美国纽约华尔街 (Wall Street)，因为牛代表乐观主义者；熊则代表悲观主义者，又据说熊要发动攻击的时候，双眼会向下看，因此就被用来比喻股市下跌的倾向。

在被认定为"熊市"之前，股市会跌破几个支撑点 (support points) 而向下探底。之后，若反弹 (rebound) 向上回升，则有可能进入盘整，甚至能突破几个压力点 (resistance points) 而转为乐观的"牛市"。

对话范例

Rob Gardener walks into the office and finds Josie Gleason reading the newspaper.

Josie: Rob, did you read the newspaper today?

Rob: No, Josie. Why? What's up?

Josie: It seems the stock market has plummeted[1] again.

Rob: Oh, no! Not again! How many points did it lose this time?

Josie: One hundred.

Rob: Let's see . . . That's three percent. Well, **there goes** the money I was hoping to use to buy a new car.

Josie: Before you get upset, I think you should look at the stock listings[2] for today.

Rob: What for?

Josie: Well, some stocks actually gained,[3] especially telecom[4] stocks.

Rob: Telecom? Let me see that newspaper. You're right! We went up five percent overnight! That's a small fortune!

Josie: For now, anyway. It may plunge[5] tomorrow.

Rob: You're right. I'm going to call my broker[6] and **cash in** all my stocks. I'm not going to **take** any **chances** with my savings.

Josie: You're wiser than some people I know. Sometimes, it's better to **play it safe**.

---

1. plummet [ˈplʌmɪt] v. 快速落下；骤然猛跌
2. stock listings [ˈstɑk ˌlɪstɪŋz] 股票盘面；股价
3. gain [gen] v. 增加
4. telecom [ˈtɛləˌkɑm] n. 电信 (= telecommunication)
5. plunge [plʌndʒ] v. 猛跌
6. broker [ˈbrokə] n. 经纪人；代理人

中文翻译　　　　　　　　　　　　　　TRANSLATION

罗伯·嘉登纳走进办公室，看到乔西·格利森正在看报纸。

Josie: 罗伯，你今天看报纸了吗？

Rob: 还没，乔西。为什么这么问？发生了什么事？

Josie: 看来股市又大跌了。

Rob: 哦，真惨！别再跌了！这次跌了几点？

Josie: 100 点。

Rob: 我看看……跌了 3%。唉，我原本打算买新车的钱飞了。

Josie: 先别难过，我想你应该先看一下今天的股价。

Rob: 为什么？

Josie: 嗯，事实上有些股票涨了，特别是通信股。

Rob: 通信股？让我看一下报纸。你说得没错！我们的股票一夜之间涨了 5%！我发了一笔小财！

Josie: 目前是如此。明天可能会大跌。

Rob: 你说得对。我要打电话给我的证券交易员，叫他把我所有的股票都卖掉换成现金。我不想再拿自己的存款冒险了。

Josie: 你比我认识的一些人要聪明。有时候稳当一点比较好。

there goes (something) （某事物）没了；消失

这是个口语用法。通常是因为情况有所改变，使得原本预期可以得到的事物落空了，就可以用这句话来表达失望。

● The city just passed the bill for the nuclear power plant, so **there goes** the neighborhood!

那个城市刚通过了核电厂的兴建案，所以邻近地区的地价就一落千丈了！

cash in 换现；兑现

指将有价值的货物、票据、股票等换成现金，实现获利。

● We **cashed in** half of our bonds to take a much-needed vacation.

我们很需要度假，所以把一半的债券拿去换成现金。

take chances 冒险；碰运气

chance在此是"危险；风险"的意思，等于risk。take chances是"冒险一试；碰运气"的意思。

● Let's **take a chance** with this new kid. I have a feeling he has a nose for this business.

我们就让这个新人试试。我觉得他对这个行业的直觉很敏锐。

play it safe 慎重行事

口语中用此来表达"不冒险；慎重行事"之意。

● We should **play it safe** and take a taxi to the meeting. We don't want to be late.

我们应该谨慎一点，搭出租车去会场。我们不想迟到。

GIVE IT A TRY!

Listening Comprehension

Listen to the conversation and answer the following questions.

1. *a.* ☐ He read it earlier today.

   b. ☐ He read it at three o'clock.

   c. ☐ He didn't read it today.

2. *a.* ☐ One hundred.

   b. ☐ One thousand.

   c. ☐ One thousand and two hundred.

3. *a.* ☐ To buy a new house.

   b. ☐ To buy a new car.

   c. ☐ To buy a new motorcycle.

4. *a.* ☐ The stock market has gone down before.

   b. ☐ Rob has enough money for a new car.

   c. ☐ The paper didn't mention the stock market.

结婚
GETTING MARRIED

婚礼

美国人的婚礼通常在称为 wedding chapel 的小教堂中举行，虽不像英国皇家婚礼的富丽堂皇，但也别有一番人情味。

传统仪式中，当音乐响起时，新郎（groom）与伴郎（best man）会先一起走进会场，接着是花童、伴娘（bridesmaid），最后再由新娘（bride）挽着父亲的右臂，缓步从教堂的红地毯走到讲台前，牧师（priest）会牵起新娘的手交给新郎。接着经过牧师的见证，新人就念誓词（oath）、交换结婚戒指（wedding ring），然后新郎就可以亲吻新娘（kiss the bride）。而婚礼举行过后，通常会在新娘家举行婚礼宴会（wedding reception），一般是在户外以茶点招待宴请来宾，除了让大家自由享用外，也可在广阔的空间里，享受热闹欢愉的庆祝气氛，有时会配上轻柔的背景音乐，或是节奏轻快的舞曲，令宾主尽欢。

婚宴结束后，新人会坐上挂满空瓶的车子，车窗上则写着"新婚"（Just Married），然后就出发去度蜜月（honey-moon），享受一段属于两个人的甜蜜时光。

DIALOGUE

Chris Black, a Sun Tech employee, is getting married. He is telling Diane, one of his coworkers, about it.

Chris: Hey, Diane, I have some great news!

Diane: Really? What?

Chris: I'm getting married!

Diane: Congratulations! Who's the lucky woman?

Chris: Her name is Amelia Stone. We've been dating for about two years now.

Diane: Oh, I didn't know you were **seeing** anyone.

Chris: Well, sometimes I like to keep my personal life private[1] to avoid office gossip.[2] Anyway, the wedding's at the end of next month.

Diane: That's **kind of** soon. Do you think you'll have enough time to make all the preparations?[3]

Chris: Yes. We're planning a small wedding. This will be the second marriage for the both of us, so we're only inviting family and a few close friends.

Diane: Oh, that sounds like it'll be really nice.

Chris: And, of course, all my colleagues[4] here at the office are invited, too.

Diane: I guess that means I'm on the guest list.[5]

Chris: Absolutely. I hope you can come and help us celebrate.

Diane: I love weddings. I **wouldn't** miss it **for the world**.

---

1. private [`praɪvɪt] *adj.* 私人的；不公开的
2. gossip [`gɑsəp] *n.* 闲言闲语
3. preparation [ˌprɛpə`reʃən] *n.* 准备
4. colleague [`kɑlig] *n.* 同事；同僚
5. guest list [`gɛst ˌlɪst] 受邀名单；宾客名单

中文翻译　　　　　　　　　　　　　TRANSLATION

太阳科技的员工克里斯·布雷克就要结婚了。他正在把这件事告诉同事黛安。

Chris: 嗨，黛安，我有个好消息！

Diane: 真的吗？什么事？

Chris: 我要结婚了！

Diane: 恭喜你！那位幸运的女士是谁？

Chris: 她叫艾米莉亚·斯通。我们已经交往将近两年了。

Diane: 哦，我不知道你在跟谁交往。

Chris: 嗯，有时候我不想让自己的私生活曝光，以免办公室里闲言闲语。总之，婚礼就定在下个月月底。

Diane: 那挺快的。你觉得你来得及准备好一切吗？

Chris: 可以。我们打算办场简单的婚礼。因为我们都是第二次结婚，所以我们只想邀请家人和一些好友参加。

Diane: 哦，那听起来好像会很棒。

Chris: 当然，办公室所有的同仁也会收到请帖。

Diane: 我想那就是说我也在受邀名单之中了。

Chris: 那当然。希望你能来帮我们庆祝。

Diane: 我喜欢婚礼。我绝对不会错过的。

学习重点

see (someone) 与（某人）交往

这是美式口语中特有的用法，用see来表示"（和某人）交往"，与date同义。

- I have only been **seeing** her for six months, but I have a feeling that one day we will be married.

  虽然我跟她才交往6个月，但我有种预感，有一天我们将会结婚。

kind of 有一点

这是相当口语化的表达，类似的说法还有sort of、a little bit。

- The market is **kind of** hot right now. We should probably wait before buying back additional shares.

  股市现在有点过热。我们最好等一阵子再买回更多的股票。

not for the world 绝对不会

这是一种夸张的说法，字面上是"即使用全世界交换都不要"，也就是"绝对不会"的意思。

- I **won't** hurt you **for the world**.

  我绝不会伤害你的。

听力小测验

Listening Comprehension

Listen to the conversation and answer the following questions.

1. a. ☐ Next year.
   b. ☐ Next month.
   c. ☐ Next week.

2. a. ☐ Amelia Stone.
   b. ☐ Emily Smith.
   c. ☐ Amanda Steward.

3. a. ☐ College classmates.
   b. ☐ A few close friends.
   c. ☐ Previous coworkers.

4. a. ☐ A small wedding.
   b. ☐ A big wedding.
   c. ☐ An office wedding.

生小孩
HAVING A BABY

保姆

美国的夫妇若需要同时上班，或同时外出，如晚间出门一起去看电影或参加宴会，就会请临时保姆（baby-sitter）来照顾自己的小孩，通常是邻居或是亲戚中较大的孩子。因此，很多女中学生和高中生都会定期充当保姆（babysit）来打工赚钱，不过现在这类工作倒也不只局限于女生才能做。费用标准依小孩的年龄、人数和时长的不同来决定。如果是长期照顾婴儿的女人，则称之为 nanny。美国有一部影集，片名就叫 *THE NANNY*，描写在富豪之家担任保姆的女主角，和其家庭成员包括男主人、秘书、男管家以及三个小孩之间的趣事，中文译名为《天才保姆》。而 nanny 在小孩子的口中，也可以指奶奶或外婆（grandmother）。

Ed Waters is an employee in Sun Tech's sales department. His wife is going to have a baby. Today, a coworker, Mary Benson, approaches[1] him in the office.

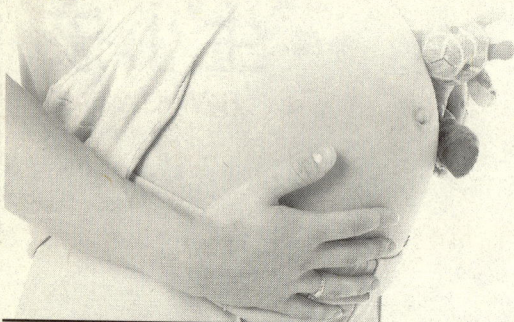

Mary: Ed, I hope your wife is free this Saturday afternoon.

Ed: Why? What's up?

Mary: Some of us from the office have planned a **baby shower** for her at my house.

Ed: A baby shower! Oh, you shouldn't have!

Mary: We're all excited about this baby. **Any word on** whether it's a boy or a girl?

Ed: According to the sonogram,[2] it's a girl.

Mary: A girl! How exciting! Listen, being a new parent is a lot of work, and we want you to know that we're **here for** you.

Ed: That's really kind of you. I am a little afraid of how tough[3] it's going to be.

Mary: You might consider hiring a nanny.[4] I did after my daughter was born. She helps me with the babysitting, the cooking, house-cleaning—all that kind of stuff.[5]

Ed: Well, with both of us working full-time, we'll need the extra help. I just hope we can find a nanny that's suitable.

Mary: I'll give you the number of the agent who found our nanny.

Ed: Thanks!

---

1. approach [ə`protʃ] v. 接近；靠近
2. sonogram [`sɑnəˌgræm] n. 超声波扫描
3. tough [tʌf] adj. 艰辛的；难缠的
4. nanny [`nænɪ] n. 保姆；奶妈
5. stuff [stʌf] n. 事物；物品

中文翻译

艾德·瓦特斯是太阳科技销售部的员工。他的妻子快要生小孩了。今天，一个同事玛丽·班森走过来。

Mary: 艾德，我希望你太太这个星期六下午会有空。

Ed: 为什么？什么事？

Mary: 我们办公室的一些同事已经计划好在我家帮她办个准妈妈派对。

Ed: 准妈妈派对！哦，你们实在不用这么大费周章！

Mary: 孩子的事让我们都很兴奋。知不知道是男孩还是女孩？

Ed: 根据超音波扫描，是个女孩。

Mary: 女孩！真令人兴奋！对了，刚开始为人父母会有很多事要忙，我们希望你知道我们都会支持你的。

Ed: 你们大家真好。我有点害怕以后会很辛苦。

Mary: 你也许可以考虑请个保姆。我女儿出生之后我就请过。她会帮我带小孩、煮饭、整理家务——那一类的杂事。

Ed: 嗯，我俩都是做全职工作，会需要多一点帮助。我只希望能找到适合的保姆。

Mary: 我会给你帮我找保姆的那位中介的电话。

Ed: 谢谢！

学习重点

baby shower 准妈妈派对

shower [`ʃaʊə] 是指"为待嫁新娘或准妈妈所举行的送礼会"。baby shower 就是"朋友们为即将到来的小宝宝准备礼物，送给待产的妈妈所开的送礼庆祝会"。

- At a **baby shower**, friends of the expectant mother all give presents for the new baby.

  在准妈妈派对上，准妈妈的朋友们都会送礼物给即将出生的小宝宝。

any word on (something) 有没有（某事的）消息

word 在此等于 news，表示"消息"的意思。所以 any word on (something) 是表示"有没有听说（某事）；有没有（某事的）消息"。

- **Any word on** who got the new position in Sales?

  有没有听说谁获得了销售部的新职位？

here for (someone) 支持或帮助（某人）

也可以说成 there for (someone)，字面上是指"在（某人）身边"，用来表达当某人有困难时会给他安慰、支援或协助的意思。

- I know this project is making your life hectic. I'm **here for** you if you need anything.

  我知道这个计划让你忙得团团转。你如果有什么需要，我都愿意帮忙。

听力小测验   **GIVE IT A TRY!**

Listening Comprehension

Listen to the conversation and answer the following questions.

1. a. ☐ A baby shower.
   b. ☐ A surprise party.
   c. ☐ A checkup.

2. a. ☐ A boy.
   b. ☐ A girl.
   c. ☐ Unknown.

3. a. ☐ At the woman's house.
   b. ☐ At Ed's house.
   c. ☐ Unknown.

4. a. ☐ How delightful it's going to be.
   b. ☐ How expensive it's going to be.
   c. ☐ How tough it's going to be.

下班后的
人际交往
SOCIALIZING AFTER WORK

生日派对

孩子的生日派对（birthday party）通常都会邀请要好的同学和朋友来参加，父母则会预先准备好生日蛋糕（birthday cake），上面用鲜奶油（cream）或巧克力酱（chocolate syrup）写上过生日的人的名字和"生日快乐"等字样，并插着比实际岁数多一支的蜡烛（candle），以表示 one to grow on，不过这可不是以虚岁来计算，而是希望在今后一年里也能健康地成长。唱完生日快乐歌（happy birthday），小寿星可以许愿（make a wish），然后把蜡烛一口气全部吹灭。

小孩子在吃完蛋糕后，通常会玩一些游戏，如大风吹（musical chairs）；至于年轻女孩子则比较喜欢彻夜不眠的睡衣聚会（slumber/pajama party）。

对话范例　　　　　　　　　　　　　　DIALOGUE

It is very late. Josie convinces[1] Sam Palmer to stop working and go out for a bite to eat. But she actually has other plans.

Sam: Looks like it's closed.

Josie: No, it's not. Let me try . . . After you.[2]

Crowd: Surprise! Happy Birthday, Sam!

Sally: Blow out the candles. I thought Josie would never pull you away[3] from the office.

Sam: Josie, you sly[4] fox. You **set** me **up**.

Josie: I had to. Otherwise it would've taken a natural disaster[5] to get you out of there at a **decent hour**.

Sam: Thanks, everyone. This is quite a surprise. And you must have called my mother.

Sally: How did you know?

Sam: She always gets my birthday confused with my sister's.

Josie: You mean, it's your sister's birthday today?

Sam: Yeah. Mine is in a month. But . . . but hey, we've got good food, good friends, and a very nice cake here. **One excuse is as good as any** to celebrate. To my sister!

Crowd: To your sister! Cheers![6] Cheers!

---

1. convince [kən`vɪns] *v.* 说服
2. after you [ˌæftə `ju] 你先请 (礼让对方先走时的用语)
3. pull away [`pʊl ə`we] 拉走；拉开；(车辆) 开走
4. sly [slaɪ] *adj.* 狡猾的
5. disaster [dɪ`zæstə] *n.* 灾害；灾难
6. cheers [tʃɪrs] *int.* 干杯 (敬酒时的用语)

中文翻译　　　　　　　　　　TRANSLATION

时间很晚了。乔西说服山姆·帕姆尔下班休息，出去吃点东西。
但是实际上她还有其他的计划。

Sam: 店好像关了。

Josie: 不，没有关。我来试试看……你先请。

Crowd: 大惊喜！山姆，生日快乐！

Sally: 吹蜡烛吧。我还以为乔西永远没办法把你拉出办公室
呢。

Sam: 乔西，你好狡猾。你陷害我。

Josie: 我不得不这么做，不然恐怕要等到发生天灾才能让你
在工作时间离开办公室。

Sam: 谢谢各位。这真令我惊讶。你们一定是打了电话给我
妈。

Sally: 你怎么知道？

Sam: 她老是把我的生日和我妹妹的搞混。

Josie: 你的意思是，今天是你妹妹的生日？

Sam: 对啊，我的生日还有一个月。但是……嘿，这里有好
吃的、好朋友，和一个很棒的蛋糕。只要有借口庆祝
就行了。就敬我妹妹吧！

Crowd: 敬你妹妹！干杯！干杯！

学习重点

set (someone) up 陷害（某人）

这是个口语用法，set (someone) up表示"陷害（某人）；诬陷（某人）"。而set up这个短语还有很多其他的意思，可以表示"设置；树立；约定"，也可以表示"成家；开业"，例如：set up shop表示"自行开业"。

● I told Jim he was coming in to a barbecue, but we were actually going to make him work. I **set** him **up**.

我叫吉姆过来烤肉，但是事实上我们是要叫他来工作。我骗了他。

decent hour 一般正常时间

decent [`disṇt ] "合理的；可接受的"。decent hour指的是"一般人可接受的正常时间；合理的时间"。反义词为obscene hour，指的是"相当晚的时间"。其中obscene [ əb`sin] 表示"过分的；下流的；可恶的"。

● Please return home at a **decent hour**.

请在正常时间回家。

one excuse is as good as any 真是个好借口

as good as表示"和……几乎一样；实际上等于"。此语有点挖苦的味道，因为既然"这个借口跟任何借口一样好"，事实上就是"根本不需要借口"或"这只不过是个好听的借口"。

● A: They said that they didn't send the shipment because they lost the order form.

他们说因为订单不见了，所以没有送货。

B: One excuse is as good as any.

真是个好借口。

听力小测验

Photographs

You will hear statements about a picture. Choose the one statement that best describes what you see in the picture. The statements will be spoken only one time.

Ans: _____

Ans: _____

职业女性
WORKING WOMEN

白领一族

职业女性（working women）又称为 career women 或 career girls。她们往往比男士们要多一些负担，必须能协调来自工作与家庭两方面的压力，否则常会落得两面不讨好的局面，而在工作上表现得特别突出的女性，则常被称为"女强人"。

现在有很多家庭是夫妻都在工作的双职工家庭（two-paycheck family），称为 DEWK（dual employed, with kids）。另外，现在的年轻夫妻也越来越流行不生孩子，保持经济宽裕的状态，以享受悠闲自在的生活，称为"丁克族"，也就是 DINK（double income, no kids），又作 DENK（double employed, no kids）。

另外，目前还有一些新兴的群体，例如：所谓的"单身贵族"、"科技新贵"、"粉领新贵"等。

DIALOGUE

Mary Kline is at a new restaurant late at night when she strikes up[1] a conversation with a waitress.

Mary: I'm so glad that you guys are open **around the clock** now.

Waitress: Yeah, you wouldn't imagine the amount of people that come in here for dinner, even in the middle of the night.

Mary: I always knew I wasn't alone. You know, it's pretty hard working and raising a family. It's nice to know that I can **stop in** here **on the way** home and get a bite to eat.

Waitress: I know how you feel. I'm a grad student[2] in my last year, working on my thesis.[3]

Mary: Wow, you must be really busy, juggling[4] work and school.

Waitress: I don't have any kids, but I think I can imagine what that's like. Sometimes, it's hard enough just balancing[5] work and school.

Mary: Well, I guess we all just do what we've got to do.

Waitress: And have a little fun on the way. Otherwise, what's the point?

Mary: You've got that right.

Waitress: So, what'll it be?

---

1. strike up [`straɪk `ʌp] 开始谈话；结交（朋友等）
2. grad student [`græd ˌstjudṇt] 研究生
3. thesis [`θisɪs] n. 论文
4. juggle [`dʒʌgl] v. 巧妙地处理；变戏法
5. balance [`bæləns] v. 使平衡；平衡

夜深时，玛丽·克莱思在一家新餐厅和一位女服务生聊了起来。

Mary: 真高兴你们现在24小时都在营业。

Waitress: 对啊，你绝对想不到即使到了半夜还有很多人会来这里吃晚餐。

Mary: 我就知道不是只有我这样。你知道吗，工作的同时又要养家真的很难。能在回家路上过来吃点东西真好。

Waitress: 我能了解你的感受。我是个研究生，今年是最后一年，我正在赶论文。

Mary: 哇，要在工作和课业之间取得平衡一定很忙。

Waitress: 我没有小孩，但是我可以想象得到你的难处。有时候光是要在工作和学业上取得平衡就已经够难的了。

Mary: 嗯，我想我们都只是在尽自己的本分。

Waitress: 还有在过程之中享受一点点乐趣，不然这还有什么意思呢？

Mary: 你说的对。

Waitress: 那，你要点什么呢？

学习重点

around the clock 夜以继日；24小时无休

直译为"绕着时钟跑"，也就是 24 hours a day（一天 24 小时无休）。

- We must keep the factory running **around the clock** to finish by the end of the month.

  如果我们要在月底前完成，工厂就必须24小时赶工。

stop in 顺道拜访；留在屋里

stop in 这个短语有两个意思，在文中是表示"顺道作短暂的拜访"，等于 stop by；而 stop in 还有另一个意思是指"留在屋里；深居简出"。

- If you are in Chicago, **stop in** and see us.

  如果你在芝加哥，就顺道过来看看我们吧。

on the way 在……的路上；在……的过程中

也可说成 on (one's) way，后面接地点，表示"在往（某地）的路上"；也可抽象地指"在（做某事）的过程中"。另外，(something) is on the way 的意思则是"（某事）正在进行中"。

- I have had a lot of fun with this company and I have made some good friends **on the way**.

  我在这家公司里度过了很多愉快的时光，也在这个过程中结交了一些好朋友。

听力小测验　　　　　　　　　GIVE IT A TRY!

Photographs

You will hear four statements about a picture. Choose the one statement that best describes what you see in the picture. The statements will be spoken only one time.

Ans: _____

Ans: _____

Ans: _____

安排会面
SETTING UP A MEETING

商务约会

在商场上，安排正式的约会之前，通常需与对方预约 (make an appointment)，查看彼此的行程表 (schedule) 后定下时间。

正式的开会叫 meeting，国际型的大会议则是 convention 或 conference，而开会的会议室可称为 assembly room 或 council chamber。会议内容原则上不超出以下范围：简报 (presentation)、讨论 (discussion)、协商 (negotiation) 和协调 (coordination) 这几项。

至于一般男女的约会应该用 date 这个词，或者说 go out with (someone)，与一般商场上约会的用语不同，可不要弄错了。

对话范例 DIALOGUE

Drew Barry calls Josie Gleason to arrange a meeting.

Drew:	Hello, Miss Gleason. This is Drew from ITC.
Josie	Hello, Drew. What can I do for you?
Drew:	I'm calling **on behalf of** my boss, Susan Goldman. She's expanding[1] the **product line**, and she'd like to set up[2] a meeting with you.
Josie:	All right. Does Susan have anything specific[3] in mind?
Drew:	She'd really like to introduce some of the latest, yet affordable[4] DVD players on the market.

Josie: We have a wide range[5] of models **right up that alley**. When would she like to get together?

Drew: She was hoping to get together at the end of this week, if possible. She wants to get going on this right away.

Josie: Let me check my schedule.[6] Yes, I'm available anytime on Friday.

Drew: How about ten o'clock in the morning at your office?

Josie: Ten o'clock sounds fine. I'm looking forward to seeing her on Friday.

Drew: Thank you. Good-bye.

---

1. expand [ɪkˈspænd] v. 拓展；发展
2. set up [ˈsɛt ˈʌp] 安排；设立；开办
3. specific [sprˈsɪfɪk] adj. 特定的；具体的
4. affordable [əˈfordəbl] adj. 负担得起的
5. range [rendʒ] n. 系列商品；一连串；范围
6. schedule [ˈskɛdʒʊl] n. 行程表；时间表

中文翻译   TRANSLATION

德鲁·贝瑞打电话给乔西·格利森安排一场会议。

Drew: 喂，格利森小姐。我是ITC的德鲁。

Josie: 嗨，德鲁。有什么我可以帮忙的吗？

Drew: 我代表我的老板苏珊·高德曼打电话给你。她想要扩展店里的产品范围，所以想和你约时间见个面。

Josie: 好的。请问苏珊有没有任何特定的构想？

Drew: 她想把一些款型最新，但售价又不会太贵的DVD播放机引进到市面上。

Josie: 我们正好有一系列非常适合的型号。她想什么时候见面？

Drew: 如果可以的话，她希望能在这个周末碰个面。她想马上着手进行。

Josie: 我看一下我的行程表。好的，星期五我整天都有空。

Drew: 约早上十点在你办公室会面如何？

Josie: 十点钟可以。我期待着她星期五的光临。

Drew: 谢谢你。再见。

学习重点

on behalf of (someone) 代表（某人）

behalf [bɪˋhæf] 的意思是"代表"，而 on behalf of (someone)
是一个惯用短语，意思是"代表（某人）；代替（某人）"，也可
用 on (someone's) behalf。

● I'll speak **on behalf of** Lisa since she's not here.

既然丽莎不在现场，我就代表她发言。

product line 产品线；产品系列

product line 是指公司所销售的所有商品。在市场上要保持竞
争力（stay competitive），除了高品质（high quality）之外，
产品线的长短、产品组合（product mix）的推出、品牌认同度
（brand recognition）如何、是否有特别优惠（special offers）
以及广告促销（promotions／advertising）等都是必须考虑的因
素。但请勿将此用语与 production line（生产线）搞混。

● Our company is introducing a new **product line** this
year.

我们公司今年将要引进一条新的产品线。

right up that alley 非常适合；内行

right up (someone's) alley 可以表示"非常适合（某人）"，因
此在本文中是指"非常适合先前所提过的那些条件"。而这个
短语的另一个意思是表示某事物"是（某人的）看家本领、拿
手好戏"。

● Basketball is **right up David's alley**.

打篮球正是大卫最拿手的看家本领。

听力小测验　　　　　　　　　　GIVE IT A TRY!

Listening Comprehension

Listen to the conversation and answer the following questions.

1. a. ☐ Susan Goldman.
   b. ☐ Josie Gleason.
   c. ☐ Susie Green.

2. a. ☐ Susan would like to introduce a new kind of DVD player.
   b. ☐ They have a wide range of similar products.
   c. ☐ The DVD players are actually very expensive.

3. a. ☐ They'll meet on Friday.
   b. ☐ They'll meet as soon as possible.
   c. ☐ They'll meet anytime today.

4. a. ☐ Negotiate the price.
   b. ☐ Call for help.
   c. ☐ Set up a meeting.

取消约定
CANCELING AN APPOINTMENT

预约

外国人相当注重"预约"的习惯,一般必须向医生、律师、美容师、大学教授等人预约,所用的词是 appointment,通常要在至少一天前先预约好时间,有些繁忙一点的"大人物"需要通过经纪人预约,还要排上一阵子才能约得到;而预约机位、旅馆房间等属于"预订的事物",则用reservation 或 booking,一般最好两天前就提前预约好。如果临时有事无法前往,也最好在前一天取消预约,以免被扣除手续费或违约金。此外,预先安排好的计划或规划,可统称为 previous engagement 或 prior engagement。

至于 engagement 这个词也会因场合不同而有不同意义,例如:engagement 用在男女双方之间的婚约,就表示"订婚";而用在物品上时,则表示"担保;抵押",相当于 pledge。

对话范例 DIALOGUE

Now, Drew must call Josie to cancel[1] the meeting he had set up.

Drew: Hello, Ms. Gleason. This is Drew of ITC. We spoke the other day.

Josie: Hello, Drew. I've prepared a nice range of samples for the meeting tomorrow morning. I think Susan will be really pleased[2] with the selection.[3]

Drew: Actually, that's the reason I called. Something urgent has **come up**. I'm afraid we have to cancel the meeting with Susan tomorrow.

Josie: I'm sorry to hear that. Is everything all right?

Drew: It's just that our general manager is **flying in from** New York unexpectedly.[4] He wants to meet with all management staff[5] tomorrow.

Josie: I see.

Drew: She would like to postpone[6] the meeting until Monday afternoon. Would that be convenient for you?

Josie: Well, I've got a pretty full schedule on Monday, but I'd be free after four thirty.

Drew: Could we **make it** at five o'clock?

Josie: Five o'clock is good. I'll see Susan at five on Monday then.

Drew: Once again, I'm really sorry about canceling the meeting **at the last minute**.

Josie: It's no problem, really. Good-bye.

---

1. cancel [ˈkænsl] v. 取消
2. pleased [plizd] adj. 愉快的；高兴的
3. selection [səˈlɛkʃən] n. (可供挑选的) 商品；选择
4. unexpectedly [ˌʌnɪkˈspɛktɪdlɪ] adv. 突然地；意外地
5. staff [stæf] n. 全体职员
6. postpone [postˈpon] v. 延期

中文翻译　　　　　　　　　　TRANSLATION

德鲁现在必须打电话给乔西取消他之前定的会议。

Drew: 你好，格利森小姐。我是ITC的德鲁，我们前几天通过电话。

Josie: 你好，德鲁。我已经为明早的会议准备好了一系列的样品。我想苏珊看到这些产品会很满意。

Drew: 事实上，我就是为这件事打电话来的。因为发生了一件重要的突发事件，所以我恐怕得取消你和苏珊明早的会面了。

Josie: 听到这件事我很遗憾。一切还好吗？

Drew: 只不过是因为我们总经理临时要从纽约搭飞机过来。他明天想和所有主管见面。

Josie: 原来如此。

Drew: 她想把会议延到星期一下午。那时候你方便吗？

Josie: 嗯，我周一的行程排得很满，不过四点半过后就有空了。

Drew: 我们约五点可以吗？

Josie: 五点可以。那我就星期一五点和苏珊见面。

Drew: 再次向你道歉，到最后一刻才取消约会真的很对不起。

Josie: 真的没关系。再见。

学习重点

come up 发生；出现

这个短语有许多不同的意思，在此是指"发生；出现"，例如：a job vacancy has come up（有职位空缺）。

● Can we reschedule for later today? Something has **come up** at headquarters that requires my immediate attention.

我们可不可以重新安排，把时间延后一点？总公司有急事，我必须立刻处理。

fly in from 从……坐飞机过来

这种说法很生动，其他类似用法还有drive / ride in from（从……开车过来 / 骑过来）。

● Miss Jones just **flew in from** Seattle for the meeting.

琼斯小姐刚刚从西雅图搭飞机过来参加这次的会议。

make it 把时间定在

口语中make it的意思很多，除了有"赶上"、"成功"等含意外，在此指的是把时间定在（某时）。

● Let's **make the meeting** for next Monday instead.

我们把会议改定在下星期一。

at the last minute 在最后一刻；在最后关头

形容直到事情发生的前一刻才做出的决定、努力等。

● **At the last minute**, Jane changed her mind and decided not to marry Tommy.

在最后一刻，简改变了心意，决定不嫁给汤米。

GIVE IT A TRY!

Listening Comprehension

Listen to the conversation and answer the following questions.

1. *a.* ☐ To reschedule the meeting.

   b. ☐ To make an appointment.

   c. ☐ To talk to Ms. Gleason's boss.

2. *a.* ☐ Their general manager is flying in from New York unexpectedly.

   b. ☐ Their CEO is coming to have a meeting without notice.

   c. ☐ Their general manager had an accident.

3. *a.* ☐ Before four thirty.

   b. ☐ After four thirty.

   c. ☐ Unknown.

4. *a.* ☐ At four thirty.

   b. ☐ At four.

   c. ☐ At five.

拜访客户
VISITING A CLIENT

零售促销

零售店 (retail store) 是从批发商 (wholesaler) 手中整批购买货品后，在店里把商品上架 (display rack) 销售。有时为了促销商品，店家会举行一些促销活动 (promotional sales)，例如：打折 (discount)、买一送一 (buy one, get one free) 等，许多商家还会针对某些产品做重点促销，并印制优惠券 (coupon)，夹带于报刊杂志中发送，一般可以短暂提升销售量，进而开发一些潜在客户 (potential customers)。此外，一些厂商为了确保优惠价格可以直接惠及客户，而不是被中间的批发商、零售商所瓜分，便会采用一种回函退款 (mail-in rebate) 的方式来促销，通常是消费者采购了特定商品后，只要将外包装寄回公司，就会获得部分现金的回馈。

促销时，当然要注意存货的多寡，若货源充裕可随时出货，叫做 in stock；而若销货超出预期而缺货，则称为 out of stock。

DIALOGUE

Josie is visiting a customer, Dan Olson, to check on the progress of a product recently introduced at Dan's store.

Josie: I can't believe it! Your display needs to be restocked,[1] and it's only ten o'clock. These are a hit.[2]

Dan: These things are **selling like hotcakes**. But actually, Josie, these are the last of our stock. We placed an order in last week, but it still hasn't arrived yet. And this isn't the first time we've found ourselves waiting for a shipment[3] to arrive.

Josie: Seriously?![4] I'm sorry. I'll need to get the details from you, so I can **get to the root of** this. Don't worry. I'll get this **ironed out**.

Dan: Thanks. Other than that, your promotion has been great. Our sales have increased dramatically[5] since we brought these in.

Josie: I believe your numbers are the highest in the region.

Dan: Does that mean we get a special deal?

Josie: I wish! You know, I'd love to give you a better price, but I already **ran** it **by** the boss and he said this is the best we can do. And you have to admit, this is a pretty good deal.

Dan: You know I had to try.

Josie: You're a shrewd[6] businessman, Dan. I think that's why we get along so well.

---

1. restock [ˌriˈstɑk] *v.* 补充；再进货
2. hit [hɪt] *n.* 热门商品；成功
3. shipment [ˈʃɪpmənt] *n.* 运输的货物
4. seriously [ˈsɪrɪəslɪ] *adv.* 认真地；严肃地
5. dramatically [drəˈmætɪkəlɪ] *adv.* 急剧地；戏剧性地
6. shrewd [ʃrud] *adj.* 精明的；敏锐的

乔西正在拜访她的客户丹·奥尔森，看看她最近引进到丹店里的商品卖得怎么样。

Josie: 我真不敢相信！才十点钟，你的货架就需要再补货了。这些产品卖得真好。

Dan: 这些东西非常畅销。不过，乔西，事实上这已经是我们最后的一批存货了。我们上个星期就下了订单，但是货到现在都还没到。而且这已经不是我们第一次等不到货了。

Josie: 真的吗？！我很抱歉。我需要从你这里了解细节，才能找出问题的根源。别担心，我会解决的。

Dan: 谢了。除此之外，你的促销很成功。自从引入这些产品后，我们的业绩就大幅增加了。

Josie: 我相信你的销售量是这一区最高的。

Dan: 那是说我们会有特别优惠吗？

Josie: 我真希望如此！我很想给你较低的价格，但我已经和老板讨论过了，他说这已经是我们的最低价。而且你也必须承认，这是很划算的交易。

Dan: 你知道我还是得试试看。

Josie: 丹，你真是个精明的生意人，我想这就是为什么我们相处得那么融洽的原因。

学习重点

sell like hotcakes 畅销

hotcake 和 pancake 都是"薄煎饼"的意思，但在固定用法中不可互换。所以"东西很畅销"要说 sell / go like hotcakes，而形容事物"非常平坦、扁平"则要说 flat as a pancake。

- Hello Kitty dolls are **selling like hotcakes**.

  Hello Kitty 猫玩偶非常畅销。

get to the root of (something)
查出（某事）的根源

root [rut] 是"树根"，get to the root of 是借"挖到树的根部"来比喻"找出问题的根源"。

- To **get to the root of** the problem, I need to take the machine apart.

  为了要找出问题的根源，我必须把机器打开。

iron (something) out 解决（某事）

iron [`aɪən] 当动词是指"用熨斗烫平"。iron (something) out 可用来比喻"把（某事）摆平；去除（障碍）"。

- We can **iron** the problem **out** if we communicate more effectively.

  如果我们更有效地沟通，就能把问题解决。

run by (someone) 征求（某人的）意见

在口语中，run (something) by (someone) 指的是"和（某人）说明或讨论（某事）以征求其意见"。

- Can you **run** your plan **by** me one more time?

  可以和我再讨论一下你的计划吗？

Listening Comprehension

Listen to the conversation and answer the following questions.

1. a. ☐ Next week.
   b. ☐ Last week.
   c. ☐ Last weekend.

2. a. ☐ It arrived two days ago.
   b. ☐ It went to the wrong store.
   c. ☐ It hasn't arrived yet.

3. a. ☐ Get the details from the man.
   b. ☐ Get some personal information from the man.
   c. ☐ Call the marketing department.

4. a. ☐ They increased dramatically.
   b. ☐ They dropped dramatically.
   c. ☐ They stayed the same.

处理客户意见

DEALING WITH AN UNSATISFIED CUSTOMER

职场上的危机处理

职场上常常会发生紧急的事情，可能是自然灾害（natural disasters）、环境问题（environmental incidents）、职场事故（workplace accidents）、生产停滞（product failure）等等，其他可能的情况还有员工诈欺（employee fraud）、政府罚款（government fines）、员工骚动（labor unrest）、群体抗议（group protests）、罢工（strike, walkout）、法律纠纷（lawsuits）、顾客投诉（customer allegations）或是被相关单位调查（under investigation by watchdog agencies）等情况，可以说不胜枚举，而公司管理层对这些情况的处理方式，统称为 crisis management，也就是所谓的"危机处理"或"风险管理"。目前，这已成为企业管理中一项重要的项目与必修的技巧，要学会如何应对得当，才能让企业化危机为"转机"。

对话范例   DIALOGUE

Josie has just received a disturbing[1] fax and is talking to her coworker Rob about it.

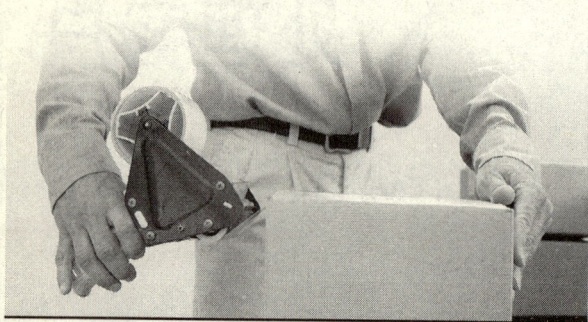

Josie: Rob! This fax just came in from ZPX. Half their order arrived defective, and they want a full refund.[2]

Rob: Oh, no! I'll get on the phone and call them right away. Do me a favor, will you? Call Shipping and find out what went wrong.

Josie: I'll **get right on it**. And I'll make photocopies[3] of this and send one on to Jake.

Rob: Not yet. Let's find out what happened first and **put it in a report**.

Josie: Good idea. But we better act quick. He should hear about it from us first.

(Later . . .)

Josie: Did you contact ZPX?

Rob: Yeah. They weren't very happy about that. But I managed[4] to convince them not to cancel the entire order.

Josie: Good for you! Shipping admitted that it was their fault. Forms got **mixed up** and the shipment went out lightly packaged.[5]

Rob: Jake's going to be furious[6] about that. We lost a lot of money on this deal.

Josie: Not to mention our reputation.[7] Jake's going to **hit the roof**!

---

1. disturbing [dr`stɜbɪŋ] *adj.* 令人忧虑的；令人不安的
2. refund [`ri‚fʌnd ] *n.* 退款（作动词时为 [ rɪ`fʌnd]）
3. photocopy [`foto‚kɑpɪ] *n.* 影印本；拷贝
4. manage [`mænɪdʒ] *v.* 设法达成；管理
5. package [`pækɪdʒ] *v.* 包装；捆扎
6. furious [`fjʊrɪəs] *adj.* 狂怒的；大发雷霆的
7. reputation [‚rɛpjə`teʃən] *n.* 名誉；名声

中文翻译　　　　　　　　　　TRANSLATION

乔西刚刚收到一份很棘手的传真，正在和她同事罗伯讨论这件事。

Josie: 罗伯！我刚刚收到这份ZPX公司的传真，他们说收到的货有一半毁损，要求全额退款。

Rob: 哦，真糟糕！我马上打电话给他们。帮我个忙好吗？打电话给货运部，查看看是什么问题。

Josie: 我马上去。而且我会把这份传真复印几份，送一份去给杰克看。

Rob: 别急，我们先弄清事情的原委，写进报告里。

Josie: 好主意，但是我们动作要快。他应该先从我们这里听到消息。

(稍后……)

Josie: 你和ZPX公司联系了吗？

Rob: 是的。他们对那件事不太满意。但是我还是设法说服了他们不要取消整笔订单。

Josie: 做得好！货运部承认是他们的疏忽。因为表格弄混了，所以商品只是稍微包装一下就发货了。

Rob: 杰克一定会很生气。这笔交易我们损失了不少钱。

Josie: 更别提我们信誉的损失了。杰克一定会气得跳脚！

学习重点

get right on it 马上做或处理

这是遇到紧急状况，需要马上处理时常用的说法，right 在此意思等于immediately，表示"立刻；马上"。

● Jack asked me to fix this; I'll **get right on it**.

杰克要我修好这个；我会马上去做。

put (something) in a report 将（某事）列入报告

report [rɪˋpɔrt] 可指"书面或口头的报告"，report on (something) 表示"对（某事的）报告或说明"。

● Please **put** this problem **in a report**.

请将这个问题列入报告。

mix up 弄混；弄乱

mix up 可以表示"使混乱，搞混了"，等于confuse；还可以表示"误认"，例如：mix A up with B表示"把A误认为B"。

● I always **mix** those two **up** because they're identical twins.

他们两个是同卵双胞胎，所以我老是把他们搞混。

hit the roof 大发雷霆

这是个夸张说法，roof是指"屋顶"。气到会撞到屋顶，当然是"很生气；大发雷霆"的意思。

● Uncle Joe **hit the roof** when he found out that Pete crashed the car.

乔叔叔发现彼特把车子撞坏时大发雷霆。

GIVE IT A TRY!

Listening Comprehension

Listen to the conversation and answer the following questions.

1. *a.* ☐ Call customers.
   b. ☐ Call the shipping department.
   c. ☐ Call the supervisor.

2. *a.* ☐ Jake.
   b. ☐ ZPX.
   c. ☐ The shipping manager.

3. *a.* ☐ Most of their order arrived defective.
   b. ☐ All of their order arrived defective.
   c. ☐ Half of their order arrived defective.

4. *a.* ☐ Find out what happened.
   b. ☐ Talk to the supervisor.
   c. ☐ Call the police.

议价
NEGOTIATING PRICES

商业往来

在职场上的商业用语包含一些专有名词，尤其在与外商交易时，最好先做一下准备，以免一时反应不过来。

通常对方会先询价（make an inquiry），然后针对该价钱议价（bargain）。如果价钱谈妥，对方则会要求报价（request for a quote，简称RFQ），并下订单（purchase order，简称PO）。完成交易后，则由卖方（vendor）开出发票（invoice）给买方，以作为凭证。

对话范例　　　　　　　　　DIALOGUE

Kelly Moss is negotiating the price of producing Sun Tech's new product with Lester Baldwin, the manager of the company that will manufacture the product.

Lester:　Considering the design of the product and the high quality of materials[1] you require, **the lowest I'd go** is three US dollars apiece.

Kelly:　That seems a little high to me. We need a **target price** of two dollars and fifty cents each to be able to **meet** our budget **requirements**.

Lester:　If you would consider using cheaper materials, I think we could go down[2] to a price of two dollars and seventy cents apiece.

Kelly:　Two seventy is still pretty high. I've talked to some other manufacturers[3] and they're able to offer me a better deal.[4]

Lester: We have the best reputation in the business for quality and on-time delivery.

Kelly: That's why I came to you first.

Lester: Our competition may be able to meet your target price, but I doubt they can meet your quality expectations[5] and delivery requirements. We can.

Kelly: Well, we're not willing to compromise on quality, so if you're willing to come down to two sixty-five, using materials that meet our quality standards,[6] I think we'd have a deal.

Lester: OK. **You've got a deal.**

Kelly: Great! Let's see how we can get things started.

---

1. material [mə`tɪrɪəl] *n.* 材料；原料
2. go down [ˌɡo `daʊn] 降低
3. manufacturer [ˌmænjə`fæktʃərə] *n.* 制造厂商
4. better deal [`bɛtə ˌdil] 更好的交易；更低的价格
5. expectation [ˌɛkspɛk`teʃən] *n.* 期望
6. standard [`stændəd] *n.* 标准

中文翻译

凯利·摩斯正在和即将承包生产太阳科技新产品的制造商经理莱斯特·鲍德温进行议价。

Lester: 考虑到这个产品的设计和你们要求的高品质原料，我最低只能算你们每件2美元。

Kelly: 那对我来说好像有点贵。我们的目标是每件单价2.5美元，这才符合我们的预算。

Lester: 如果你考虑用便宜一点的原料，我想每件可以降到2.7美元。

Kelly: 2.7还是很高。我和其他几家厂商谈过，他们可以给我更低的价格。

Lester: 我们在这个行业里信誉卓著，品质佳且运送准时。

Kelly: 这就是为什么我会先来找你。

Lester: 我们的竞争对手也许可以开出符合你们期望的价格，可是我怀疑他们能否符合你们对于品质的期望以及运输上的需求。但是我们可以。

Kelly: 嗯，我们不愿意在品质上打折扣。所以，如果你们能把价格压到2.65美元，并使用品质达到我们标准的原料，我想我们就成交了。

Lester: 好吧，一言为定。

Kelly: 太好了！我们来讨论该如何开始吧。

学习重点

---

the lowest I'd go 我最低出价……

此语是用来表示给对方一个最低的价格（lowest / best price），go在此是sell for（卖）的意思。

● My car runs very well, so **the lowest I'd go** is five thousand.

我的车跑起来很顺，所以我最低只能卖你5 000。

---

target price 目标价格

指厂商或某人心中所预先设定好的价格。

● It might be difficult to reach a **target price** of five dollars per piece.

要达到每件5美元的目标价格可能会有困难。

---

meet requirements 符合需求

meet在此表示"满足；符合；达到"。

● I'm sorry, but these designs don't **meet** our **requirements**.

很抱歉，但这些设计并不符合我们的需求。

---

you've got a deal 成交

在商场上表示"成交"，日常生活中表示"一言为定"，也可以说成 it's a deal。

● A: I'll sell you the computer at a discount price How about it?

这台电脑我给你折扣价如何？

● B: **You've got a deal**.

成交。

听力小测验　　　　　　　　　　GIVE IT A TRY!

Listening Comprehension

Listen to the conversation and answer the following questions.

1. a. ☐ They have the best reputation in the business for quality and on-time delivery.

   b. ☐ They have the best reputation in the business for quality and real-time delivery.

   c. ☐ They have the best reputation in the business for quality and discounts.

2. a. ☐ Two dollars and sixty-five cents apiece.

   b. ☐ Two dollars and fifty cents apiece.

   c. ☐ Two dollars and seventy cents apiece.

3. a. ☐ Quality expectations and delivery requirements.

   b. ☐ Budget requirements.

   c. ☐ Budget and delivery requirements.

4. a. ☐ Two dollars and sixty-five cents apiece.

   b. ☐ Two dollars and fifty cents apiece.

   c. ☐ Two dollars and seventy cents apiece.

参加商务招待会

ATTENDING A BUSINESS RECEPTION

卡片的 **3** 大种类

卡片虽小，但作用可不小，适度地使用，常能发挥意想不到的功效。常见的有以下几类：

❶ 名片 (business card)：

上面印有公司名称 (company)、姓名 (name)、头衔 (title)、地址 (address)、电话 (phone number) 及电子邮件地址 (e-mail address) 等，一般在初次见面自我介绍的时候使用。

❷ 访客卡 (calling card)：

指拜访时交给秘书或装在礼物中的名片，也叫做 visitor card。

❸ 贺卡 (greeting card)：

有生日卡 (birthday card)、周年纪念日贺卡 (anniversary card)、送别卡 (bon-voyage card)、祝贺卡 (congratulatory card)、祝早日康复卡 (get-well card)、邀请卡 (invitation) 及感谢卡 (thank-you card) 等等。

对话范例 ·

Josie and a new salesman, Jimmy Lin, are at a reception.[1] Josie gives Jimmy some tips on how to make the most of his time there.

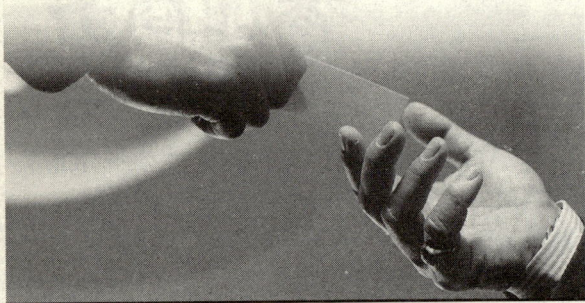

Jimmy: I've been waiting for this reception all week. I can't wait to get some of my own leads.

Josie: Smart thinking. But why do you have all those brochures?[2]

Jimmy: The party ends at two. I figure I can have them all distributed[3] by one thirty.

Josie: No, no, no, no. Let me **clue** you **in**. These brochures will make you look like the **new kid on the block**.

Jimmy: What should I do, then?

Josie: Hand out business cards.[4] That's it. This room is filled with potential[5] clients, but the unwritten law[6] is, you leave your work at the door.

Jimmy: But how am I supposed to get anything out of this if we can't talk business?

Josie: You have business cards. Just get a card for a card.

Jimmy: Then follow up on Monday?

Josie: You catch on quick. Let's split up[7] so we can **cover** more **ground**.

Jimmy: Great idea. This is going to be **a walk in the park**. I'll meet you back here at two.

---

1. reception [rɪ`sɛpʃən] *n.* 招待会
2. brochure [bro`ʃʊr] *n.* 小册子
3. distribute [dɪ`strɪbjut] *v.* 分发；分配
4. business card [`bɪznɪs ˌkɑrd] 名片
5. potential [pə`tɛnʃəl] *adj.* 潜在的
6. unwritten law [ʌn`rɪtn ˌɔlɔ] 不成文规定
7. split up [`splɪt ˌʌp] 分开

乔西和一个新业务员吉米·琳参加一场招待会。乔西教吉米一些利用时间把握机会的诀窍。

Jimmy: 我整个星期都在等这次招待会。我等不及想为自己找到一些机会。

Josie: 很聪明。但是你拿着那些广告手册做什么？

Jimmy: 宴会两点结束。我想一点半之前我就能把这些全部发完。

Josie: 不，不，不，不。我来告诉你吧。带着这些手册会让你看起来像是菜鸟。

Jimmy: 那我该怎么做？

Josie: 递名片。那样就够了。这里到处都是潜在的客户，但有项不成文规定：别把工作带进门。

Jimmy: 但是如果我们不谈生意，那我来这里有什么好处？

Josie: 你带了名片来啊。和别人互换名片就好了。

Jimmy: 然后星期一再联络？

Josie: 你学得真快。我们分头进行，覆盖到的范围会比较大。

Jimmy: 好主意。这应该会像在公园里散步一样简单。我两点再回这里和你碰面。

学习重点

---

clue (someone) in 提示（某人）

clue (someone) in 表示"给（某人）消息或提示，让其进入状态"。类似的短语还有 fill (someone) in、give (someone) the lowdown。

- Why don't you **clue** your partner **in** about the non-smoking rule?

  为什么你不告诉你的同伴不准抽烟的规矩？

---

new kid on the block 菜鸟；没经验的人

字面上的意思为"街上新搬来的小孩"，引申为"新人、新面孔；没经验的人"的意思。

- Hey, there's the **new kid on the block**. Let's go meet her.

  嘿，有个新人在那边。我们去和她见见面。

---

cover ground 覆盖范围

ground 原指"地面"，这里用来指任何范畴的事物，cover ground 是指"覆盖到某范围；完成某部分"。

- It's three o'clock and we still have a lot of **ground** to **cover**.

  已经三点了，我们还有很多事尚未完成。

---

a walk in the park 轻而易举之事

字面上是指"在公园散步"，用来形容某件事再简单不过。意思近似 a piece of cake、a breeze、a snap 等。

- This project is going to be **a walk in the park**.

  这项计划将会易如反掌。

听力小测验 GIVE IT A TRY!

Listening Comprehension

Listen to the conversation and answer the following questions.

1. *a.* ☐ He wants to distribute them to potential clients.

   b. ☐ He wants to read them before he goes on a trip.

   c. ☐ He doesn't know where to put them.

2. *a.* ☐ By two.

   b. ☐ By one thirty.

   c. ☐ By one.

3. *a.* ☐ The new kid on the block.

   b. ☐ An old hand at marketing.

   c. ☐ An old hand at sales.

4. *a.* ☐ Hand out the brochures.

   b. ☐ Go home.

   c. ☐ Get a card for a card.

送礼物
GIVING GIFTS

消费中的 6 种客户

"客户"这个词在英文中有许多不同的说法：

❶ shopper：到商店买东西的人。这是通用的说法。

❷ customer：到某家店去买东西的人。这是从商家（merchant）的角度来看。另外，buyer 和 purchaser 也都可以用来表示类似于 customer 的意思。

❸ consumer：意思是"消费者"，属于正式用法。在报章、杂志及学术文章中，经常会使用到。

❹ client：一般是指寻求如法律事务所、银行及电脑维修等专业服务的人；或是指商业中的买方。相对地，卖方则称为 vendor。

❺ guest：到旅店投宿的人，基于服务业"以客为尊"的宗旨，称之为饭店的"宾客"。

❻ passenger：搭乘车、船、飞机等交通工具的人，也就是"乘客"。

对话范例　　　　　　　　　　　**DIALOGUE**

Mike Turner and Mary Bennett have spent the week in town meeting with Sun Tech. They are now saying good-bye to Sam Palmer.

Mike: Thank you for your hospitality[1] these past few days.

Sam: It's been our pleasure. I feel our time has been well spent.

Mary: As soon as we get back to New York, we'll write up the new contracts, and send them to you express.[2]

Sam: Sounds great.

Mary: Oh, and we got **a little something** for your staff. Could you see that they get it?

Mike: And please thank them for their hard work and extra effort they have shown in making this week go so smoothly.

Sam: My pleasure. This is very thoughtful[3] of you.

Mary: We would also like to give you a **token of** our **gratitude**.

Sam: You didn't need to **go to such trouble**!

Mike: You are very modest.[4] That is one of the reasons why we enjoy doing business with you.

Sam: The feeling is mutual.[5] I look forward to your next visit. Have a good flight back.

Mike: Thank you.

---

1. hospitality [ˌhɑspɪˈtælətɪ] *n.* 好客；招待
2. express [ɪkˈsprɛs] *adv.* 用快递寄送
3. thoughtful [ˈθɔtfəl] *adj.* 体贴的；替他人着想的
4. modest [ˈmɑdɪst] *adj.* 谦虚的
5. mutual [ˈmjutʃuəl] *adj.* 互相的；彼此的

中文翻译

麦克·特纳和玛丽·班尼特一整个星期都在和太阳科技会谈。现在他们要向山姆，帕姆尔道别。

Mike:　　谢谢你们这几天以来的热情招待。

Sam:　　这是我们的荣幸。这几天我感觉很充实愉快。

Mary:　　我们一回到纽约就会把新合约拟好，然后用快递寄给你们。

Sam:　　听起来很不错。

Mary:　　哦，我们还准备了一些小礼物要送给贵公司的职员。能不能请你帮忙交给他们？

Mike:　　也请代为感谢他们这个星期以来的辛苦以及格外的付出，才使事情进行得如此顺利。

Sam:　　乐意之至。你们想得非常周到。

Mary:　　我们也想送你一份薄礼聊表谢意。

Sam:　　你们不必如此费心！

Mike:　　你太客气了。这就是我们喜欢和你谈生意的原因之一。

Sam:　　彼此彼此。期待你们下次再度光临。祝你们一路顺风。

Mike:　　谢谢你。

学习重点

a little something 不是什么很贵重的东西

这是送礼给别人时的谦虚用语，表示"并不是什么很贵重的东西，不成敬意"。但如果是别人送你礼物，你可不要说a little something。

- A: Your father has **a little something** for you for your graduation.

  你爸爸买了一点东西当你的毕业礼物。

  B: Keys? Oh, Dad! You bought me a brand-new car?! Wow, thanks!

  钥匙？哦，爸！你买了一辆新车给我？！哇，谢了！

token of gratitude 聊表心意

token [`tokən] *n.* 象征
gratitude [`grætə‚tjud] *n.* 感谢

token of gratitude 表示"所送的礼物是作为谢意的象征"。

- Please accept this **token of gratitude** on behalf of the entire staff.

  请代表所有员工收下这份聊表心意的礼物。

go to such trouble 大费周章

指某人花费了很多精力或心思在某件事物上。

- He **went to such trouble** to get us into a really nice hotel. We should express our thanks with a gift.

  他如此尽心尽力地为我们找了一间非常好的旅馆。我们应该送点礼物表示感谢。

听力小测验　　　　　　　　　GIVE IT A TRY!

Listening Comprehension

Listen to the conversation and answer the following questions.

1. a. ☐ Write a report.
   b. ☐ Write up the new contracts.
   c. ☐ Send an e-mail.

2. a. ☐ Their hard work and extra effort.
   b. ☐ Showing up late.
   c. ☐ The new marketing plan.

Question and Response

You will hear a question or statement and three responses. Choose the best response to the question or statement. They will be spoken only one time.

1. _____   2. _____   3. _____   4. _____

安排出差期间的商务会议
ARRANGING AN OUT-OF-TOWN BUSINESS MEETING

旅行知多少

一般出门旅行称为travel。

例 After five years of foreign **travel**, he finally came back. 在国外旅行5年之后，他终于回来了。

在一段时间内旅行经过的一段路程，则称为journey。

例 It's a long **journey** by train from Paris to Moscow. 从巴黎搭火车到莫斯科是一段很长的旅程。

"海上或空中的旅行"为voyage。

例 The **voyage** from London to Stockholm used to take months.
以前从伦敦航行到斯德哥尔摩需要花上好几个月。

若要专指"海上旅行"，可用cruise。

例 Tom is going on a round-the-world **cruise**.
汤姆正在进行海上巡游，环游世界。

而短暂的旅行，则叫做trip。

例 How was your **trip** to New York?
你的纽约之行如何？

对话范例

Jerry Evans received an invitation to a client's **grand opening**. He plans to be in the area anyway, so he calls the client, Bob Roberts, to arrange a meeting.

Jerry: Hello, Bob. Jerry Evans, here. I got your message about the grand opening.

Bob: Hi there, Jerry. Do you think you'll be able to make it?

Jerry: **It just so happens** that I have a conference[1] in Washington that very week.

Bob: What a coincidence![2] Do you think you'll have time to **break away** from your meetings?

Jerry: Your message said that the doors open on Saturday . . . Listen, I'm finished with my conference on Friday afternoon. Could we meet Friday evening?

Bob: That would be great. Then I can **fill you in on** Saturday's activities. Jerry, are your accommodations[3] all set, or can I help?

Jerry: Oh, that's already covered. But would you mind arranging transportation[4] for me to the airport on Saturday evening?

Bob: Not a problem.

Jerry: Thanks, I appreciate it. Right now I've got a ten p.m. flight.[5] Will that leave enough time for us to get through what we need to?

Bob: It's perfect.

Jerry: Great! OK, see you then.

---

1. conference [ˈkɑnfərəns] 研讨会；大型会议
2. coincidence [koˈɪnsədəns] 巧合
3. accommodations [əˌkɑməˈdeʃənz] 住宿
4. transportation [ˌtrænspəˈteʃən] 交通；运输
5. flight [flaɪt] 班机；班次

中文翻译 | TRANSLATION

杰瑞·伊凡斯受邀参加一个客户的开幕典礼。他本来就计划要
到那个地区去，所以他打电话给那个客户鲍伯·罗伯斯安排
会面。

Jerry: 喂，鲍伯。我是杰瑞·伊凡斯。你那条关于开幕典礼
的留言我收到了。

Bob: 嗨，杰瑞。你有办法到场吗？

Jerry: 那个星期我在华盛顿刚好有个研讨会。

Bob: 真巧！你能从会议中抽个空吗？

Jerry: 你留言里说星期六开业……这样吧，星期五下午我就
开完会了，我们能不能星期五晚上见个面？

Bob: 那太好了。那我就可以把星期六活动的情况先告诉你
了。杰瑞，你食宿都安排好了吗？还是要我帮忙？

Jerry: 哦，已经安排好了。不过，你能不能帮我安排星期六
晚上到机场的交通工具？

Bob: 没问题。

Jerry: 谢谢，很感谢你的帮忙。目前我打算要乘坐晚上十点
钟的飞机，这样的话，时间才够把我们要做的事情做
完吗？

Bob: 太完美了。

Jerry: 太好了！好，那就到时候见啦。

学习重点

---

grand opening 开幕典礼；开幕仪式

习惯上，公司新开张用 grand（盛大的），听起来比较有气势。要注意的是，有些翻译中常用 new opening 表示新开幕，但这并不正确，可能是源自洋泾浜英语。

- During the supermarket's **grand opening**, the staff gave away free samples.

  在那家超市开幕期间，店员们分发了免费的试用品。

---

it just so happens 非常碰巧

形容事先没有经过安排，却恰好发生的事情。

- A: Hello, I'm calling about the sales position.

  喂，我是打电话来应征销售员的。

  B: Sorry, **it just so happens** that we filled that position today.

  抱歉，我们今天刚好有人补上了这个位置。

---

break away 离开；脱身

break away 原为"逃脱"之意，在此则指"离开；脱离"，通常与介系词 from 连用，其后再接宾语。

- I'm so busy these days. I can't **break away** from my desk for even fifteen minutes!

  我这几天好忙，连离开桌子 15 分钟都不行！

---

fill (someone) in on (something) 将（某事）告诉（某人）

用来表示"为（某人）转达一些其错过的信息等"。

- Will someone please **fill** me **in on** the presentation? I apologize; I was late.

  有没有人能告诉我简报的内容？抱歉，我迟到了。

听力小测验

Listening Comprehension

Listen to the conversation and answer the following questions.

1. a. ☐ The grand tour.
   b. ☐ The grand opening.
   c. ☐ The grand station.

2. a. ☐ Wall Street.
   b. ☐ Washington.
   c. ☐ Wales.

3. a. ☐ He has a conference there.
   b. ☐ His girlfriend is there.
   c. ☐ He was invited by Bob.

4. a. ☐ On Sunday.
   b. ☐ On Friday.
   c. ☐ On Saturday.

预订航班
与旅馆房间

MAKING AIRLINE AND HOTEL
RESERVATIONS

4种功能性的饭店旅馆

一般的饭店旅馆称为 hotel，而 motel 是指"汽车旅馆"，是提供给开车旅行者住宿的旅馆，备有停车位，但房间设施较为简单，使旅客以较低廉的价格，解决吃住的问题。resort 则是提供度假者居住的饭店或别墅，一般设施较豪华，使顾客能完全放松心情、享受假期。一般来说，hotel还可就功能性分为以下4种：

❶ airport hotel：位于机场附近的旅馆，方便转机的旅客短暂住宿。

❷ casino hotel：位于拉斯维加斯或里诺等赌城的饭店，饭店内附设有赌场，还有节目表演，多以豪华著称。

❸ residential hotel：提供长期住宿的旅馆，多位于医院附近。

❹ commercial hotel：最普遍的商业旅馆，大多会提供办公桌椅及上网服务等，甚至有无线宽带上网设施。

Sally Jenkins calls Ken Rogers, a travel agent, to make travel arrangements for Sam Palmer.

Ken: Horizon Travel. May I help you?

Sally: Hello. This is Sally Jenkins. I'd like to **book** hotel and airline **reservations** for my boss. He's attending an electronics[1] trade show in Las Vegas at the end of the month.

Ken: Can I get his full name,[2] please? And will he be traveling alone?

Sally: His **surname** is Palmer, P-A-L-M-E-R, and his first name is Sam. Yes, he'll be traveling alone.

Ken: Will that be a **one-way** or a **round-trip ticket**?

Sally: Round-trip.

Ken: And what are his **travel dates**?

Sally: He plans to leave on the tenth and return on the sixteenth. Concerning the hotel, if there is a three-star[3] hotel located downtown available, that would be great.

Ken: OK, let me check the computer . . . I can book his flight reservation right now, but I need to check on the hotel reservation and call you back later.

Sally: No problem. My number is 658-0266, extension 5-1-3. And I'll be expecting your call.

---

1. electronics [ɪˌlɛkˋtrɑnɪks] *n.* 电子产品；电子学
2. full name [ˋfʊl ənem] 全名
3. three-star [ˋθriəstɑr] *adj.* 三星级的

中文翻译 　　　　　　　　　　　　　　　TRANSLATION

莎莉·简金斯打给旅行社业务员肯·罗杰斯,帮山姆·帕姆尔安排旅行事宜。

Ken: 地平线旅行社,有什么可以为您服务的吗?

Sally: 你好,我是莎莉·简金斯。我想替上司订机票和旅馆房间。他这个月月底要到拉斯维加斯参加一场电子会展。

Ken: 可以告诉我他的全名吗?还有,他是一个人去吗?

Sally: 他姓帕姆尔,P-A-L-M-E-R,名字是山姆。没错,他是一个人去。

Ken: 要单程票还是往返票?

Sally: 往返票。

Ken: 他什么时候去,什么时候回来?

Sally: 他打算10号启程,16号回来。关于饭店方面,如果有市区三星级的饭店,那是最好了。

Ken: 好的,让我查一下电脑……我现在可以马上帮他订机位,但是旅馆订房的事我还得查一下,稍后再打电话给您。

Sally: 没问题。我的电话是658-0266,分机513。我会等你的电话。

学习重点

book a reservation 预订；预约

需要预订的事物通常有 book airline / car / hotel reservations（订机位 / 订车 / 订旅馆房间）等。

● Oh, no! I forgot to **book** hotel **reservations**!

哦，糟了！我忘了预订旅馆房间！

surname 姓氏

美国人的名字分三个部分：名字＋中间名＋姓。姓是 surname 或 last / family name。名字是 first / given / Christian name。而中间名为 middle name。

● Please write your **surname** on this line.

请把你的姓写在这条线上面。

one-way ticket、round-trip ticket 单程票、往返票

美国人说单程票是 one-way ticket，往返票是 round-trip ticket；而英国人则分别说 single ticket 和 return ticket。

● How much is a **round-trip ticket** from Beijing to Shanghai?

北京到上海的往返票要多少钱？

travel dates 行程日期；旅游日期

一般旅行社在帮客户订机票或旅馆房间时，常需要知道客户的行程日期。dates 用复数是因为包含了出发和回来的日期。

● The travel agent got my **travel dates** wrong on my tickets, so I have to return to her office.

旅行社的人把我机票上的往返日期弄错了，所以我得再到她的办公室一趟。

听力小测验   **GIVE IT A TRY!**

Listening Comprehension

Listen to the conversation and answer the following questions.

1.   *a.* ☐ Book hotel and airline reservations.
     b. ☐ Arrange a meeting.
     c. ☐ Cancel a meeting.

2.   *a.* ☐ Attend a computer exhibition.
     b. ☐ Attend an electronics trade show.
     c. ☐ Attend a movie opening.

3.   *a.* ☐ Yes, he will.
     b. ☐ No, Sally will go with him.
     c. ☐ Yes, he will be traveling with Josie.

4.   *a.* ☐ Leave on the sixth and return on the sixteenth.
     b. ☐ Leave on the fifth and return on the fifteenth.
     c. ☐ Leave on the tenth and return on the sixteenth.

提早下班
GETTING OFF EARLY

商店种类

一般的小商店叫 shop 或 store，而有些商店则有习惯叫法，如咖啡店 (coffee shop)、修理店 (repair shop) 或药房 (drugstore)、书店 (bookstore)、杂货店 (grocery)；另外，还有美容中心 (beauty salon)、美发沙龙 (hair salon) 等。

较大型的商店称为超市 (supermarket) 或百货公司 (department store)。最大型的卖场或购物中心称为 shopping center 或 shopping mall，由许多商店组成，并带有大型停车场。

美国地大物博，一些新型的购物中心里，甚至还设有美术馆 (art gallery)、剧场 (theater)、电影院 (cinema)、医院 (hospital)、银行 (bank)、邮局 (post office)、饭店 (hotel) 等周边设施，犹如一座城镇般方便，吃喝玩乐一应俱全。

Sandra Shoemaker, one of Josie Gleason's customers, needs to leave early to see the dentist. Her coworker, Al Goodman, agrees to help her out.

Sandra: I've been trying to see my dentist all week, but he's completely **booked up**.

Al: What's wrong?

Sandra: I think I have an abscessed[1] tooth.

Al: You shouldn't **mess around** with that. You should see my dentist. Her schedule's pretty flexible.[2] Here, try her number.

(Later . . .)

Sandra: Al, she'll see me first thing[3] after lunch. It could be an in-and-out[4] procedure, but if it isn't, can you cover[5] for me this afternoon?

Al: Sure. I'll cash out⁶ and close up shop. Anything else?

Sandra: Yes. I'm expecting a call from Ms. Gleason. If she does call, go ahead and schedule our second appointment for tomorrow. My appointment book is on my desk.

Al: Do you really think you'll be able to make it tomorrow? Maybe you should **shoot for** Monday, just to be safe.

Sandra: Yeah, **good thinking**. OK, I'd better go. I don't want to be late! Thanks for your help, Al!

Al: It's no big deal. Hope it goes well!

---

1. abscessed [`æb͵sɛst] *adj.* 肿的；长脓疮的
2. flexible [`flɛksəbl] *adj.* 有弹性的
3. first thing [`fɝst `θɪŋ] 一开始做的事
4. in-and-out [`ɪnənd`aut] *adj.* 快速的；暂时的
5. cover [`kʌvɚ] *v.* 暂代替某人的工作
6. cash out [`kæʃ] [`aut]（一个营业日结束时）结账

中文翻译　　　　　　　　　　　　　TRANSLATION

桑德拉·修梅克是乔西·格利森的客户之一。她要早点下班去看牙医。她的同事艾尔·古德曼答应帮她忙。

Sandra: 这一个星期以来，我一直想要去看牙医，但他已经预约满了。

Al: 怎么了？

Sandra: 我觉得我有颗牙齿好像发炎了。

Al: 这可不能开玩笑。你应该去找我的牙医看看，她的时间很有弹性。来，打她电话试试看。

（稍后……）

Sandra: 艾尔，她说午餐后帮我第一个看牙齿。应该会很快，但是如果有拖延，你今天下午能不能帮我代班？

Al: 当然可以。我会把账结好，并把店关好打烊。还有其他事吗？

Sandra: 有。我在等格利森小姐的电话。如果她打过来，就直接跟她敲定我们明天第二次会面的时间。我的约会时间记事本放在桌上。

Al: 你觉得你明天真的可以吗？保险起见，也许你应该排在星期一才对。

Sandra: 对啊，还好你想到了。好啦，我得走了。我可不想迟到！艾尔，谢谢你的帮忙！

Al: 这没什么。希望一切顺利！

学习重点

book up 预约满额

book 在此指"预订"，而 up 表示"完全地；彻底地"，因此加起来表示"预订一空"。其他结构类似的用语还有 eat up（吃光）、use up（花光）和 run up（用光）等。另外，预约满额也可说成 booked solid。

● Our factory is **booked up** for the whole summer. We'll have to stop taking orders.

我们工厂整个夏天的订单都预约满了。我们不能再接订单了。

mess around 随便应付；轻视

此语还有"闲逛；浪费时间"的意思，在此是指"随便应付；打马虎眼；不当一回事"。

● We don't have time to **mess around**. Let's get straight to the point here.

我们没有时间打马虎眼了。直接说重点吧。

shoot for 定下目标

在口语中，shoot for 指"定下目标，努力去达成"。

● Let's **shoot for** a May deadline. That should give us enough time to finish our research.

我们的截止日期就定在 5 月，这样我们应该有足够的时间可以完成我们的研究。

good thinking 还好你想到了

人总有考虑不够周详的时候，当别人替你想到一些你没注意到的事情时，便可用此语来赞扬对方。

● **Good thinking**, John. I didn't even think about that.

约翰，还好你想到了。我根本没想到那一点。

听力小测验 GIVE IT A TRY!

Listening Comprehension

Listen to the conversation and answer the following questions.

1. a. ☐ She can't get an appointment.
   b. ☐ Her dentist closed up the clinic.
   c. ☐ She doesn't have any free time.

2. a. ☐ The woman should call again.
   b. ☐ The woman should wait for another week.
   c. ☐ The woman should see his dentist.

3. a. ☐ Close up shop for her shop.
   b. ☐ Call customers for her.
   c. ☐ Attend a meeting for her.

4. a. ☐ Mrs. Gleason's.
   b. ☐ Mr. Gleason's.
   c. ☐ Ms. Gleason's.

请假一天
ASKING FOR A DAY OFF

假期类别

have a day off 表示"休假或请假一天";长一点的假期则用 holiday 或 vacation 来表示,但这两个词在美国和英国的意思并不相同。美国人用 vacation 表示"假期";holiday 则指"法定假日"。而英国人以 holiday 表示"假期";vacation 则专指"学校的寒暑假期"。

此外,一般公务人员或军人请假,英文是 go on leave,例如:sick leave 表示"病假";on leave 则表示"休假中"。

另外,在口语中,他们也常用动词短语 get away 来表示"外出度假";这个短语原本有"逃离"的意思,因此引申为远离工作环境,到外面去放松、休息一番,以便能够精力充沛地回到岗位,重新出发。欧美国家很早就实施每周休两天以及年假制度,让员工在努力工作之余,也可以得到充分休息。

DIALOGUE

Jenny Donaldson, a saleswoman[1] at Sun Tech, is asking her manager, Jake Lancer, for a **day off**.

Jenny: Mr. Lancer, do you have a minute?

Jake: Certainly. What's up?

Jenny: I have some **personal business** I need to take care of, and I was wondering if I could have Friday off.

Jake: Is it important? Because, you know, we are very busy.

Jenny: Well, I'm moving this weekend, and I need to arrange for utilities[2] at the new apartment.

Jake: But the deadline for your marketing report[3] is Friday. Management is having a big meeting to go over it.

Jenny: Yes, I know. And I've been working really hard to complete[4] it.

Jake: But will it be ready in time for the meeting?

Jenny: I'll be **more than happy to** work overtime this week to see that the report is ready and on your desk—before Thursday.

Jake: Well, if you can guarantee[5] that the report will be ready in time for the meeting, you can have Friday off.

Jenny: Thanks a lot, Mr. Lancer.

Jake: You're welcome, and good luck with your move.

---

1. saleswoman [ˈselzˌwumən] *n.* 女业务员；女店员
2. utility [juˈtɪlətɪ] *n.* 公用设施（水电、煤气等）
3. report [rɪˈpɔrt] *n.* 报告
4. complete [kəmˈplit] *v.* 完成
5. guarantee [ˌgærənˈti] *v.* 保证；承诺

中文翻译 TRANSLATION

太阳科技的业务员珍妮·唐纳森正要向她的经理杰克·兰瑟请假一天。

Jenny: 兰瑟先生，你有空可以谈一下吗？

Jake: 当然。什么事？

Jenny: 我有一些私事要处理，不知道星期五我可不可以请个假？

Jake: 是很重要的事吗？你知道的，我们现在很忙。

Jenny: 嗯，我这周末要搬家，我得安置一下新公寓里的设备。

Jake: 但是你的营销报告的截止日期就是星期五。管理部要开个重要会议详细审查这个报告。

Jenny: 是的，我知道。我正一直努力把它完成。

Jake: 但是你赶得及在开会前完成吗？

Jenny: 我很愿意这星期加班以便如期完成报告，交到你桌上——在星期四之前。

Jake: 好吧，如果你能保证报告能在会议前如期赶出来，那你星期五就可以请假。

Jenny: 真谢谢你，兰瑟先生。

Jake: 不客气，祝你搬家顺利。

学习重点

day off 请假；休假

day off用来表示请假或休假。我们通常会在day off前面加上日期、数字来表示休假时间的长短。

● On my last **day off**, I spent the afternoon playing tennis with a couple of friends.

上次休假，我整个下午都在和几个朋友一起打网球。

personal business 私事

也可说成personal matters，而business affairs则是指"公事"。

● Joy won't come into work this week for **personal business** reasons. I think there was a death in her family.

乔伊因为有一些私事，这个星期不会来上班。我想是因为她家里有人去世。

more than happy to V. 很乐意去（做某事）

more than happy字面上是"不只是乐意"，也就是"非常愿意"的意思。这样的说法会让听的人感到很高兴，因为这表示你是很乐意去做某事，一点都没有强迫感。

● I would be **more than happy to** help you look up those statistics for your report.

我会很乐意帮你查找报告中所需要的统计资料。

听力小测验

Listening Comprehension

Listen to the conversation and answer the following questions.

1. a. ☐ Stay at home and spend time with her family.
   b. ☐ Finish the report she's doing for her boss.
   c. ☐ Take care of some things for her new apartment.

2. a. ☐ A utilities report.
   b. ☐ A management report.
   c. ☐ A marketing report.

3. a. ☐ Saturday.
   b. ☐ Thursday.
   c. ☐ Friday.

4. a. ☐ Work overtime.
   b. ☐ Take the work home.
   c. ☐ Do it next week.

劳动关系
EMPLOYER-EMPLOYEE RELATIONS

上班族的一周

美国实施每周休两日制度，但每到星期一开工时，上班族（nine-to-fiver）常会显得精神不济，工作情绪低落，这种情形我们称之为 blue Monday，表示"忧郁的星期一"；星期三则称为小周末，一般工作也不会太认真。

到了星期五，办公室就开始弥漫着周末狂欢的气息，大家无心工作，以致有 T.G.I.F.（Thank God It's Friday）这个口语用法。所以，一个星期中真正认真工作的时间，就只剩下星期二和星期四了。

对话范例   DIALOGUE

Sam is upset because his subordinates[1] have been arriving late for work. He is talking to his assistant, Sally Jenkins, about it.

Sally: You seem upset, Sam. Is anything wrong?

Sam: I'm getting concerned[2] because so many staff have been showing up[3] late for work.

Sally: It's true. A lot of people have been coming in late. They probably think you don't mind.

Sam: Maybe it's because I hang out[4] with a lot of them outside the office.

Sally: They must see you more as a buddy[5] than a boss. It's because you're so friendly.

Sam: You're right. They don't view me as an authority figure[6] anymore. And I'm afraid they don't respect me as a boss.

Sally: So what are you going to do about it?

Sam: Starting today, I'm going to **lay down the law**. From now on, everyone in the company must follow regulations **to a tee**.

Sally: I'll post a notice ASAP. What should it say?

Sam: No more punching in late. No more **clocking out** early. No more calling in sick without a good reason or without a **doctor's excuse**.

Sally: Anything else?

Sam: No more personal phone calls or e-mails on company time!

Sally: All right. I'll get right on it!

---

1. subordinate [sə`bɔrdṇɪt] *n.* 部属；下属
2. concerned [kən`sɜnd] *adj.* 忧虑的；忧心的
3. show up [`ʃo `ʌp] 出现；出席
4. hang out [`hæŋ `aut] 闲逛
5. buddy [`bʌdɪ] *n.* 好朋友；兄弟；伙伴
6. authority figure [ə`θɔrətɪ `fɪgjə] 权威人士（在此指高层主管）

中文翻译　　　　　　　　　　　　　　TRANSLATION

因为下属近来常常迟到，山姆很不高兴。他正在和他的助理莎莉·简金斯谈起这件事。

Sally: 山姆，你好像不太高兴。有什么问题吗？

Sam: 有这么多员工上班都时常迟到，我开始有点担心。

Sally: 的确。近来很多人上班常迟到。他们可能以为你不在意。

Sam: 可能是因为我下班后常和他们在一起休闲娱乐。

Sally: 他们一定是把你当兄弟看，而不当上司看。因为你太和蔼可亲了。

Sam: 你说得对。他们不再把我当作主管看待。而且恐怕他们也不尊重我这个上司。

Sally: 那你现在要怎么处理这件事？

Sam: 今天开始，我要严格规定。从今以后，公司里的每个人都必须严格遵守规定。

Sally: 我会尽快贴张公告。上面要写些什么？

Sam: 上班打卡不准迟到。不准早退。没有正当理由或医生证明，不准打电话来请病假。

Sally: 还有其他的吗？

Sam: 上班时间不准再打私人电话或收发私人的电子邮件！

Sally: 好的。我马上去办！

lay down the law 立下规矩；严格规定

字面上的意思是让别人"将所说的话都当作法律来执行"，表示要别人完全听命行事，所以此语就表示"立下规矩；严格规定"。

● The boss **laid down the law** about the dress code in the office.

老板订下办公室的着装规定。

to a tee 精确地；完全地；恰好地

也可以说成 to a T，意思是"符合每个细节，一字不差"，引申为"精确地；完全地；恰好地"的意思。

● Barry followed the operating instructions **to a tee**.

贝瑞完全遵照操作指示办事。

clock out 打卡下班

clock 在此作动词，表示"打卡"。所以 clock out 或 punch out 就表示"打卡下班"，而 clock in/on 或 punch in 则为"打卡上班"。

● It's five o'clock already. Time to **clock out**!

已经五点了。该下班了！

doctor's excuse 医生证明

这可不是"医生的借口"，而是医生所开的假条，用以证明某人因生病而无法上班、上学等。英国人称之为 sick note。

● Since Jimmy was sick yesterday, he needs to bring in a **doctor's excuse** for his absence from school.

因为吉米昨天生病没来上学，所以他今天必须带着医生证明到学校。

听力小测验 GIVE IT A TRY!

Listening Comprehension

Listen to the conversation and answer the following questions.

1. *a.* ☐ Many staff have been showing up early for work.

   b. ☐ Many staff have been showing up late for work.

   c. ☐ Many staff have been working overtime.

2. *a.* ☐ Because he's so friendly.

   b. ☐ Because he's so young.

   c. ☐ Because he's so strong.

3. *a.* ☐ They don't see him as a buddy.

   b. ☐ They view him as an authority figure.

   c. ☐ They don't respect him as a boss.

4. *a.* ☐ He is going to lay down the law.

   b. ☐ He is going to reward them.

   c. ☐ He is going to show up late.

加薪
A SALARY INCREASE

薪资类别

美国的薪资常以年薪计算，通常每月以薪资支票（pay-check）给付，称为salary。而以星期或小时来计算的临时工（temp），其工资则称为wage，通常以现金（cash）支付。至于律师或翻译的专业服务，其酬劳则称为fee，以一小时甚至半小时为计费单位。而这些薪资对接受的一方而言，通称为income（收入）。

对支付方而言，salary只是其支出的一部分。从公司管理层来看，除了支付给职员薪资外，还需要支付劳动保险、健康保险，甚至退休金预存款等款项，因此整个人事支出并不只是所有员工的薪资（salary）总和；平均来说，大约是两倍的金额才是该项支出的实际数字。

至于薪资的真实数据，属于个人隐私（privacy），因此不应向别人询问，否则会被认为没有礼貌。

Carl Simpson is a new accountant[1] at Sun Tech. He has just finished his three-month **probationary period**. His boss, Jake Lancer, is talking to him about his salary.

Jake: Mr. Simpson, it's been **brought to my attention** that your three-month probationary period is up.

Carl: Yes, it is. I started work here on July first. I hope my work has been satisfactory.

Jake: Well, you know, there's a lot to learn when you begin working with a new organization.

Carl: There certainly is. There are so many **rules and regulations**.

Jake: I know you've been working late almost every night and coming in on Saturdays to get familiar with things. The company is very happy with your progress.[2]

Carl: That's good to know. I was beginning to think that I would never get the hang of it.

Jake: You're doing just fine. I wanted to let you know that we have approved[3] your first salary increase.[4]

Carl: That's great! Thank you!

Jake: Don't get too excited. It's only a three-percent raise.[5] But keep up the good work, and you'll get another raise in six months.

Carl: Terrific! Thank you for the incentive![6]

Jake: You're welcome.

---

1. accountant [ə`kauntənt] *n.* 会计师
2. progress [`prɑgrɛs] *n.* 进步
3. approve [ə`pruv] *v.* 赞成；通过
4. salary increase [`sælərɪ `ɪnkris] 加薪
5. raise [rez] *n.* 加薪；增加
6. incentive [ɪn`sɛntɪv] *n.* 激励；刺激

中文翻译

卡尔·辛普森是太阳科技新来的会计师,他刚满三个月试用期。他的上司杰克·兰瑟正和他谈到薪资问题。

Jake: 辛普森先生,我注意到你3个月的试用期已经满了。

Carl: 是的,没错。我是7月1号开始上班的。希望我的工作表现令人满意。

Jake: 你知道,刚开始在一家新公司上班,你要学的事情很多。

Carl: 的确没错。而且还有许多的规则和规章。

Jake: 我知道你几乎每天晚上都工作到很晚,连星期六也来上班,以便赶快进入状态。公司对你的进步感到很满意。

Carl: 真高兴听你这么说。我还以为我永远都做不好呢。

Jake: 你做得不错。我想告诉你我们已经通过给你首次加薪了。

Carl: 太好了!谢谢你!

Jake: 先别太高兴。只不过涨了3%。不过,继续好好表现,6个月后,你还可以再加一次薪。

Carl: 太棒了!谢谢你给我的鼓励!

Jake: 不客气。

probationary period 试用期

probationary [prəˈbeʃənɛrɪ] *adj.* 试用的；缓刑的

一般公司在录取新员工时，通常会告知有3个月至6个月的试用期，这样可给双方一个选择的机会。期满后，如果正式录用，通常会加薪甚或进一步签约长期聘用。类似的说法还有 on probation，但 on probation 还有"缓刑中；留校察看"等负面的意义，所以使用时要小心。

● All new employees have a three-month **probationary period**.

所有的新员工都有3个月的试用期。

bring to (someone's) attention （某人）注意到

attention [əˈtɛnʃən] 的意思是"注意；留意"。相关的常用语很多，如 attract / draw / steal (someone's) attention（吸引某人的注意）、distract (someone's) attention（分散某人的注意）、pay attention to（注意……）等。

● Kevin **brought** it **to** my **attention** that I will need a visa to enter Australia.

凯文提醒我，我需要有签证才能进入澳大利亚。

rules and regulations 规则和规章

rule 和 regulation 有细微的差别。rule 泛指一般指导或管理行为的条款或惯例，而 regulation 则是正式列入条文的法规。

● I'm not sure that I clearly understand the **rules and regulations** concerning time off. Could you explain them to me?

我对于休假的相关规定并不是很清楚，你能不能帮我解释一下？

听力小测验　　　　　　　　　　　　　　**GIVE IT A TRY!**

Listening Comprehension

Listen to the conversation and answer the following questions.

1. a. ☐ He started work on June first.
   b. ☐ He started work on July first.
   c. ☐ He started work on August first.

2. a. ☐ They approved his first salary increase.
   b. ☐ They approved his promotion.
   c. ☐ They approved his project.

3. a. ☐ Five percent.
   b. ☐ Six percent.
   c. ☐ Three percent.

4. a. ☐ In five months.
   b. ☐ In six months.
   c. ☐ In three months.

年终奖金
ANNUAL BONUSES

奖金与津贴

在美国，一般工薪阶层或劳动阶层并没有奖金制度，只有执行级 (executive) 或超级推销员，在业绩达到或超过配额 (quota) 要求时，才会有奖金 (bonus) 可得。

但前些年红极一时的电脑相关产业为了吸引优秀工程师或程序设计师 (programer) 来公司上班，就提供了一些 allowance 或 benefits (补助、津贴)，甚至还有分红 (bonus) 或股票认购权 (stock option) 给员工，因此每年所获得的股利盈余 (dividend) 也水涨船高，相当可观；但风水轮流转，自从高科技股指数 (如 NASDAQ 指数等) 一路下滑后，似乎他们的津贴与奖金也都缩水了。

　　　　　　　　　　　　DIALOGUE

It is the end of the year, and it is time to give out bonuses to employees. Sally Jenkins' supervisor, Sam Palmer, gives Sally her bonus.

Sam: Sally, I called you into my office to talk to you about something.

Sally: I hope everything's OK.

Sam: Actually, I'd like to personally[1] present[2] you with your annual bonus.[3]

Sally: Thank you so much.

Sam: I would like to also **take this opportunity** to tell you what a fine job you've been doing in this company.

Sally: Thank you. I've been working very hard to stay on top of my work.

Sam: And you've been doing a very good job.
I've noticed over the past year that you've
had a lot of improvement[4] in your
work.

Sally: Those training courses[5] that you asked me
to attend have really paid off.

Sam: I'm glad they have. There is one thing,
though. I'd like you to keep this bonus
confidential.[6]

Sally: OK. I understand.

Sam: Good. Bonuses are **based on** work
performance, and not everyone performed
as well as you did. I wouldn't want anyone
to find out that their bonus wasn't as much
as yours.

Sally: I understand. I won't **say a word**.

---

1. personally [`pɜsn̩lɪ] *adv.* 亲自地；就个人来说；针对个人地
2. present [prɪ`zɛnt] *v.* 给；呈献（正式用语）
3. annual bonus [`ænjʊəl `bonəs] 年终奖金
4. improvement [ɪm`pruvmənt] *n.* 进步
5. training course [`trenɪŋ ˌkors] 培训课程
6. confidential [ˌkɑnfə`dɛnʃəl] *adj.* 保密的；机密的

岁末年终，该是发奖金给职员的时候了。莎莉·简金斯的上司山姆·帕姆尔把奖金发给她。

Sam: 莎莉，我把你叫进办公室来是想和你谈一件事。

Sally: 我希望一切都好。

Sam: 事实上，我想亲自把年终奖金发给你。

Sally: 真是谢谢你。

Sam: 我也想趁这个机会告诉你，你在公司的表现很好。

Sally: 谢谢你。我很努力以便掌握所有工作的进度。

Sam: 你做得很好。我注意到过去这一年来你在工作上有很大的进步。

Sally: 你让我去参加的培训课程真的很有帮助。

Sam: 我很高兴有帮助。不过还有一件事。我希望你不要让别人知道奖金的事。

Sally: 好。我了解。

Sam: 很好。因为奖金是按照工作表现发放的，并不是每个人的表现都像你一样好。我不想让其他人知道他们的年终奖金没你高。

Sally: 我了解。我会守口如瓶的。

学习重点

take this opportunity 趁机；借这次机会

opportunity [ˌɑpəˈtjunətɪ] *n.* 机会；良机

其反义用法为 miss the opportunity（错过机会）。

● Now that we have two weeks off, we should **take this opportunity** to travel somewhere.

既然我们有两个星期的假，我们应该利用这个机会到什么地方去旅游一下。

base on 根据

base on 与 according to 时常都被译作"根据"，但两者有差别。base on 是根据"资料、事实、表现"等作出结论或证明；而 according to 根据的是"直接的引述，如某人所说、某数字所显示的或某报告所证明的"等。

● **Based on** market data, we could be facing revenue problems starting in the third quarter next year.

根据市场数据，我们明年第 3 季开始可能将面临营业收入困难的问题。

not say a word 守口如瓶；保密

字面上是"一个字也不说"，也就是"保守秘密；守口如瓶"的意思，也可说成 not breathe a word。

● Please keep in mind that this is to be a surprise announcement by our company. Do **not say a word** to anyone—even to our best clients.

请记住这件事是本公司的特别公告。千万不要泄露给任何人知道——就算是关系最好的客户也不行。

听力小测验

Listening Comprehension

Listen to the conversation and answer the following questions.

1. a. ☐ Because he wants to present her with her annual bonus in person.

   b. ☐ Because he wants to present her with her birthday gift.

   c. ☐ Because he wants to tell her about her promotion.

2. a. ☐ Sally has been doing a very good job.

   b. ☐ Sally has been late for work all the time.

   c. ☐ Sally has been absent a lot lately.

3. a. ☐ Punch in on time.

   b. ☐ Keep this bonus confidential.

   c. ☐ Work harder.

4. a. ☐ Attendance.

   b. ☐ Work performance.

   c. ☐ Sales.

离职
LEAVING A JOB

离职的申请

员工提出辞呈，英文的动词是resign；口语说法是quit或
ship out。离职前一定要事先知会雇主，一般是在离职的
一个月或两个星期前，先提出正式通知，如one month's
notice、two weeks' notice，之后再提出正式的书面辞呈
（resignation letter）。经过正当合理的手续完成辞职过
程，对员工来说也许有点麻烦，但日后还可能会有帮助。
因为应聘时有些工作需要有推荐信函（reference letter），
如果能找工作上的主管来写，可能在你应聘另一个工作
时，会有所帮助。

若是突然间离职了，则可说walk out。至于被雇主辞退，
英文是用lay off；而口语说法则是fire、sack。

关于担任特殊公职人员的"辞职、卸任或引退"，则用动词
abdicate或resign，例如：abdicate from the presidency
表示"辞任总统的职位"；resign from a board of directors
表示"退出理事会的席位"。

对话范例

Brian Albertson sits down to talk with his manager, Jake Lancer.

Brian: Good morning, Jake.

Jake: Brian, good morning! How are you doing this morning?

Brian: Good. But, uh . . . Do you have a minute to talk?

Jake: That question always **carries** some **weight**, Brian. What's up?

Brian: Well, uh . . . Here it goes . . . My wife has been promoted[1] to manager in her company.

Jake: That's great! I'm so happy for you!

Brian: Yeah, it's great for us. But . . . We have to move to Philadelphia. We have to be there by the first of next month.

Jake: Oh? This is quite a surprise, Brian. I'm sad that you'll be leaving us. You run this place with **clockwork efficiency**, you know.

Brian: But these three weeks will give us time to hire and train a replacement.[2]

Jake: Well, thanks for the notice, Brian. Assistants like you are **one in a million**. I guess we'd better start looking ASAP.

Brian: With your approval,[3] I'll put out notices[4] today and screen[5] the applicants for you.

Jake: That would be great. Schedule them in as you **see fit**. Brian, things certainly won't be the same without you around here.

---

1. promote [prə`mot] v. 使升职；增进
2. replacement [rɪ`plesmənt] n. 替代人选
3. approval [ə`pruvl] n. 同意；认可
4. notice [`notɪs] n. 公告；启事
5. screen [skrin] v. 审查；筛选

中文翻译   **TRANSLATION**

布莱恩·艾伯森坐下来和他的经理杰克·兰瑟谈话。

Brian: 杰克，早上好。

Jake: 布莱恩，早上好！你今天早上好吗？

Brian: 很好。但是，嗯……你有时间谈一下吗？

Jake: 布莱恩，你这样问一定是有什么重要的事情。怎么了？

Brian: 嗯，是这样的……我太太的公司升她当经理了。

Jake: 那太好了！我真替你高兴！

Brian: 是啊，我们都很高兴，但是……我们必须搬到费城去。下个月一号之前我们就得搬过去。

Jake: 嗯？布莱恩，这真是令人意外。听到你要离开我们，我很难过。你把这里的事情处理得井井有条。

Brian: 不过还有3周，我们有时间去找人来培训，接替我的位置。

Jake: 嗯，布莱恩，谢谢你通知我。像你这样的好助手真是万里挑一。我想我们最好尽快开始找人。

Brian: 既然有了你的同意，我今天马上发布公告，并帮你甄选应聘者。

Jake: 那样太好了！只要你觉得有合适的人选就帮我安排。布莱恩，这里没了你，情况肯定会差很多的。

学习重点

carry weight 具有重要性

weight是"重量"。carry weight若用来形容人，是指"有分量、权威；举足轻重"；用来形容事物或意见，则是指"具有重要性的；有影响力的"。

● He is not the manager, but he really **carries** some **weight** in the company.

他虽然不是经理，但在公司却有举足轻重的地位。

clockwork efficiency 非常有效率

clockwork [`klɑk،wɜk] 这个名词原本指"钟表的发条装置"，引申为"精确；精准"的意思，所以clockwork efficiency是指"非常有效率"。

● Their office runs with **clockwork efficiency**. That's why they are one of the best.

他们公司的运作非常有效率，这就是为什么他们是最好的公司之一。

one in a million 万里挑一；难得一见

一百万个之中才有一个，当然是"非常难得"。

● Don't let him go. He is **one in a million**.

别让他离开。他是难得的人才。

see fit 认为合适的或正当的

fit表"适合的"，所以see fit的意思是"认为合适的或正当的"，也可说成think fit。as (someone) see fit to do (something) 指"（某人）认为做（某事）是合适的"。

● Dad punishes the children as he **sees fit**.

父亲认为孩子不乖就是要打。

听力小测验　　　　　　　　GIVE IT A TRY!

Listening Comprehension

Listen to the conversation and answer the following questions.

1. a. ☐ Brian.
   b. ☐ Brian's wife.
   c. ☐ Brian's sister.

2. a. ☐ Washington.
   b. ☐ Philadelphia.
   c. ☐ Pennsylvania.

3. a. ☐ Two weeks.
   b. ☐ Three weeks.
   c. ☐ Four weeks.

4. a. ☐ Put out notices.
   b. ☐ Take the week off.
   c. ☐ Have a farewell party.

辞职

RESIGNING FROM A JOB

跳槽4大指南

❶ 年轻时较容易换工作；年纪一大，基于工作稳定（job security）的考虑，能保有一份稳定的工作与收入，比较而言可能会更重要。

❷ 有专业知识（specialized knowledge）或技能（skills）才有跳槽的本钱。因此最好能利用空闲时间，好好充实自己；如果有在职培训的机会，也应尽量争取与把握。

❸ 还没收到新雇主的通知前，不要辞掉目前的工作。否则成了"过河小卒"，想要回头也都没办法了。要事先做好彻底的评估以及周全的准备，再毅然决然迈出下一步。

❹ 不要过河拆桥（burn your bridges），并且要和以前公司的同事继续保持联络，也许在下一份工作中，你还会需要他们的帮助。

Amy Wood, a senior[1] accountant at Sun Tech, has found a new job. Today, she is meeting with the company president, Ned Williams, to resign.[2]

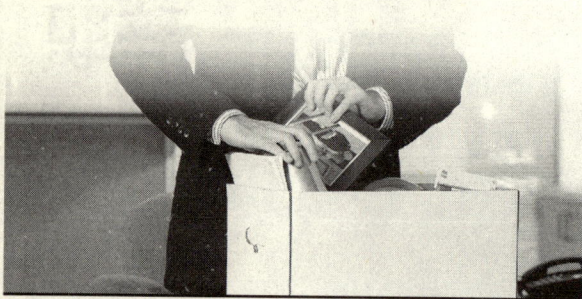

Ned: Oh! Amy, you wanted to see me?

Amy: Yes. But before I start, I want to thank you for the support[3] you've given me over the past twelve years.

Ned: Ah—but I sense[4] what you're going to tell me is something I don't want to hear.

Amy: Well, I've been offered a position at Top Flight Airlines. It's a small company, but I plan to accept the offer.

Ned: So **what you're telling me is** you wish to resign.

Amy: That's correct. I have valued[5] my experience here at Sun Tech, but I feel that it's time for me to **move on** to a position that will be a bit more challenging.

Ned: Amy, I'm sorry to hear that you'll be leaving. We're going to miss you around here, but I do understand your **position**.

Amy: I want to give you my notice today. Here's my letter of resignation. It will be effective on the fifteenth.

Ned: Amy, if necessary, could you stay on a little longer to train someone to take over[6] your position?

Amy: Of course, Mr. Williams. It's **the least** I **can do**.

Ned: Well, I do appreciate it. Thanks, Amy.

---

1. senior [ˈsinjɚ] *adj.* 资深的
2. resign [rɪˈzaɪn] *v.* 辞职
3. support [səˈpɔrt] *n.* 支持
4. sense [sɛns] *v.* 感觉到
5. value [ˈvæljʊ] *v.* 珍惜；重视
6. take over [ˌtek ˈovɚ] 接替；继任（职务）

中文翻译   TRANSLATION

艾米·伍德是太阳科技的一位资深会计师，她找到了一份新工作。今天她要向公司的总裁奈德·威廉姆斯辞职。

Ned: 哦！艾米，你想见我是吗？

Amy: 是的。但是在开始谈之前，我想先谢谢你在过去这12年来对我的照顾。

Ned: 啊——不过我感觉到你要说的事是我不想听的。

Amy: 嗯，顶尖航空公司提供给我一个职位。那是家小公司，但是我打算接受那份工作。

Ned: 所以你的意思是你要辞职。

Amy: 是的。我珍惜在太阳科技的经历，但我觉得是该换一个更具挑战性的工作的时候了。

Ned: 艾米，听到你要离开我很遗憾。我们会想念你的，但是我的确能体谅你的想法。

Amy: 今天我想正式向你告知。这是我的辞职信，15号就开始生效。

Ned: 艾米，如果有必要的话，你可不可以多待一段时间来培训接替你职位的人？

Amy: 没问题，威廉姆斯先生。这是我起码该做的。

Ned: 我非常感谢。谢谢你，艾米。

学习重点

what you're telling me is 你的意思是

此语常用来确认对方的意思。

- **What you're telling me is** that if we don't deliver by Monday, you'll cancel the entire order?

  你的意思是说如果星期一货还没到的话，你就要取消整张订单吗？

move on 转换

原本指"继续向前走"，在此用来指"转换"到下一项工作、活动或议题等，用法为 move on to (something)。

- I've really had enough of this dead-end job. It's time for me to **move on** to a position where I am respected and can earn a decent salary.

  我真受够了这个没前途的工作。是该换工作的时候了，我该找个受人尊重并且薪水又高的工作。

position 立场；想法

position 一般是指"位置；职位；姿势"，但在这里是指"立场；观点；想法"。

- Her **position** is that we spend more on advertising.

  她的看法是我们要多花点钱在打广告上。

the least (someone) can do （某人）起码该做的事

用来表示某人觉得对某事有义务，至少该帮点忙。

- You paid for dinner, so let me pay for the movie. Come on, it's **the least** I can do.

  你付了晚餐的钱，所以看电影由我来付。拜托，这是我起码该做的。

GIVE IT A TRY!

Listening Comprehension

Listen to the conversation and answer the following questions.

1. a. ☐ 12 years.

   b. ☐ 14 years.

   c. ☐ 10 years.

2. a. ☐ She's been offered a job with a major airline.

   b. ☐ She's been offered a job with a small company.

   c. ☐ She doesn't say what kind of company it is.

3. a. ☐ She thinks it's time to do something more challenging.

   b. ☐ She thinks it's time to retire and move somewhere sunny.

   c. ☐ She thinks it's time to go to another city.

4. a. ☐ On the sixteenth.

   b. ☐ On the fifteenth.

   c. ☐ On the eighteenth.

退休
RETIRING

退休计划

美国的工作福利制度包括提供一种退休账户，称为 401（k），在账户停用前，也就是离职前，每月存入的薪水并不会扣税，员工可以在离职后利用这笔钱来做投资。而如果公司没有退休福利制度，一般人会每个月固定在保险公司存入一笔钱，到退休后就有一笔退休金，叫做 pension plan。

另外，put out to pasture 在口语中也表示"退休"的意思，可不是"放牛吃草"的意思。put out 在此是 place outside（放到外面）的意思。

put out 还有 stretch out（伸出）、produce（生产）、turn off（熄灭）、extinguish（扑灭）以及 cause trouble（带来麻烦）等其他意思，所以还要视其上下文来决定意义，例如：put the match out 是表示"把火柴熄灭"的意思。

DIALOGUE

Ron Taylor has been working in the marketing department for twenty-five years. He is meeting with his current supervisor, Josie Gleason.

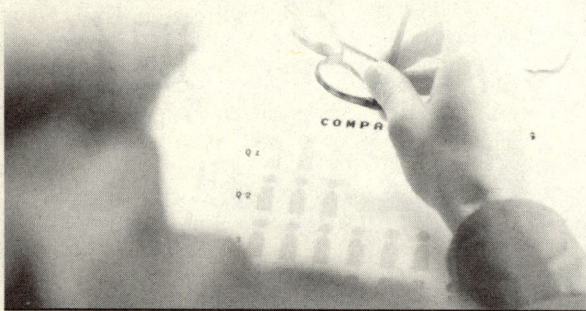

Ron: Well, Josie, I've enjoyed working for the company these past twenty-five years, but I do feel it's time for me to retire.[1]

Josie: **Has it been** twenty-five years **already**?

Ron: Well, amazingly, yes. It's funny how **time** really does seem to **fly** when you're busy working and raising a family.[2]

Josie: It sure does. I guess your children have all grown up and moved away[3] by now.

Ron: Oh. Yes, they, they have. And I want the chance to get out and enjoy life before I get too old.

Josie: Well, your service and dedication[4] to the company over the years has certainly been appreciated. We'll definitely miss you.

Ron: Oh, and I'll miss everyone here as well. But I must say I am looking forward to **doing** just **a little** relaxing, and maybe doing a little traveling as well.

Josie: That sounds like an excellent plan. You've certainly deserved[5] it.

Ron: Oh, thank you, thank you. I do plan to leave at the end of next month.

Josie: Well, that gives us plenty of time to find a replacement. Listen, if there's anything I can do for you, just let me know.

Ron: Oh, thank you, thank you. I'll certainly do that.

---

1. retire [rɪ`taɪr] v. 退休
2. raise a family [`rez ə `fæməlɪ] 养家糊口
3. move away [`muv ə`we] 搬走；离开家里
4. dedication [ˌdɛdə`keʃən] n. 牺牲；奉献
5. deserve [dɪ`zɝv] v. 应得；值得

中文翻译 TRANSLATION

罗恩·泰勒已经在营销部工作了25年，现在他正在和现任上司乔西·格利森说话。

Ron: 乔西，我很高兴过去这25年来能为公司服务，但我觉得该是退休的时候了。

Josie: 已经有25年了吗？

Ron: 是啊，是很令人惊讶。当你忙着工作、养家糊口时，时间真的过得很快。

Josie: 的确是如此。我想现在你所有的小孩都已经长大成人，离开家里了。

Ron: 嗯，是啊，他们、他们都搬走了。我想趁还没太老之前去外面走走，好好享受人生。

Josie: 嗯，真的很感谢你这些年来对公司的服务与贡献，我们一定会想念你的。

Ron: 哦，我也会想念这里的每个人。但我得说我很想休息一下，也许会去旅行一下。

Josie: 计划听起来很不错。这当然是你应得的。

Ron: 哦，谢谢你、谢谢你。我打算下个月月底离开。

Josie: 那么我们有充分的时间来找接替的人选。那，如果有什么事情我可以帮忙的，请告诉我。

Ron: 太谢谢你了。我一定会的。

学习重点

···

Has it been . . . already? 已经……了吗?

中间加上时间,表示已经过了很长时间而没发觉。

● **Has it been** twenty minutes **already**? I've barely made it through half of the topics I had hoped to cover.

已经过20分钟了吗? 我想讲的主题还没讲到一半呢。

···

time flies 光阴似箭

这是 time flies like an arrow 的缩略语,和中文成语"光阴似箭"意思相同,用来感叹时间流逝得很快。

● **Time flew** by so fast during our vacation in Bali.

当我们在巴厘岛度假时,时间过得真是快。

···

do a little (something) 做些……事

这种用法是表示做的事情只是为了消遣,而不是以严肃的心态去做。

● After I retire, I'd like to **do a little** fishing and perhaps take up painting.

在退休后,我想去钓钓鱼,或许也会开始学画画。

Listening Comprehension

Listen to the conversation and answer the following questions.

1. a. ☐ 20 years.
   b. ☐ 25 years.
   c. ☐ 30 years.

2. a. ☐ Get out and enjoy life.
   b. ☐ Work overtime.
   c. ☐ Have a family and raise some children.

3. a. ☐ Exercising.
   b. ☐ Reading.
   c. ☐ Traveling.

4. a. ☐ The man's service and deication.
   b. ☐ The man's attendance.
   c. ☐ The man's marketing reports.

解雇员工
TERMINATING AN EMPLOYEE

颜色的联想

解雇通知除了叫 pink slip 外，也可称之为 marching orders 或 walking papers。

粉红色被视为是属于女性的颜色。在美国，如果有人生了小女孩，亲朋好友就会送她粉红色（pale pink）的衣服、玩具、卡片等。而如果生的是男孩，则会送天蓝色（pale blue）的礼物。

在工作职务方面，我们常听到蓝领阶层（blue-collar worker），也就是体力劳动者；而白领阶层（white-collar worker）则是指办公人员。此外，粉领阶层（pink collar）是指秘书、女服务生、打字员等一般由女性所担任的工作。不过，随着女性就业人口的增加与男女平等意识的增强，可能要避免使用。

此外，"黑色"一般意思似乎都不太好，例如：blackmail 这个词常译为"敲诈"，除了当名词之外，也可当动词，表"敲诈；勒索"的意思。

DIALOGUE

Billy Leopold has been in the marketing department for two months, but he has not been performing well, and he has caused some problems. Now, his manager, Sam Palmer, has called him into his office.

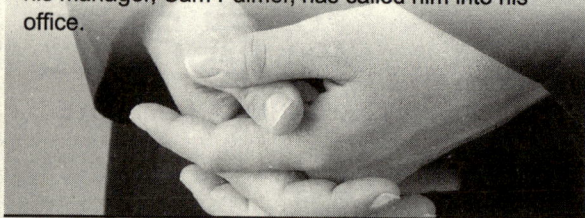

Sam: Billy, the reason I called you into my office is about your work.

Billy: Yes?

Sam: The truth is . . . I'm not very satisfied with your job performance.

Billy: I thought I was doing a good job.

Sam: Billy, you've been **reprimanded** a number of times for lateness[1] and for using company time for personal matters.

Billy: I know I've been late a couple of times; my motorcycle has been breaking down.[2] I'm sorry. I promise to do better in the future.

Sam: I'm afraid it's too late. Right now, your tardiness[3] is the least of my problems.

Billy: What do you mean?

Sam: My secretary has proof[4] that you have **misappropriated** company **funds** on several occasions. We won't be prosecuting,[5] but this simply can't be allowed.

Billy: I didn't steal any money! Your secretary is lying!

Sam: I'm sorry. It's too late. We have to let you go.

Billy: You're firing me?! Giving me my **pink slip**?!

Sam: I'm sorry it had to **turn out** this way. Your termination[6] is effective immediately.

---

1. lateness [`letnɪs] n. 迟到；迟；晚
2. break down [`brek `daʊn] 故障；损坏
3. tardiness [`tɑrdɪnɪs] n. 迟到；迟缓
4. proof [pruf] n. 证据；证明
5. prosecute [`prɑsɪ‚kjut] v. 起诉；控告
6. termination [‚tɜmə`neʃən] n. 终止；结束；解雇

中文翻译

比利·雷欧帕已经在营销部工作2个月了，但是他的表现不佳，而且造成了一些问题。现在，他的经理山姆·帕姆尔把他叫进办公室。

Sam: 比利，我叫你进办公室来是想谈谈你的工作。

Billy: 请说？

Sam: 事实上……我对你的工作表现不太满意。

Billy: 我觉得我做得不错啊。

Sam: 比利，你已经因为迟到以及利用上班时间处理私事而多次遭到惩戒。

Billy: 我知道我迟到过几次，都是因为我的摩托车坏了。我很抱歉。我保证以后会改进。

Sam: 恐怕太迟了，现在你的迟到是我最不关心的问题。

Billy: 什么意思？

Sam: 我的秘书有证据证明你曾经多次挪用公款。我们不会提出起诉，但是这种事是绝对不能宽待的。

Billy: 我没有偷钱！你的秘书说谎！

Sam: 很抱歉，太迟了，我们必须让你离开。

Billy: 你要炒我鱿鱼？！把我开除？！

Sam: 我很遗憾事情会变成这样。你的解雇立即生效。

reprimand 惩戒

reprimand是指"正式的训斥、惩戒",而scold则是指"日常生活中,老师对学生或父母对小孩等的斥责、责备"。

● I've **reprimanded** Todd twice already for the same problem.

我已经为了同样的问题惩戒托德两次了。

misappropriate funds 挪用公款

misappropriate [ˌmɪsə`proprɪˌet] v. 侵占;盗用

在此funds指"金钱;资金",作此意讲时要用复数形式。

● The secretary was charged with **misappropriating funds** from the firm.

那个秘书因挪用公司的款项而遭到起诉。

pink slip 开除通知单

在美国开除通知单都是用粉红色的纸写的,因此用pink slip来代称。此语亦可当动词用:be pink-slipped (被开除)。

● I was given the **pink slip** at my last job after only half a year.

我上次的工作做了半年就被开除了。

turn out 结果变成

其后可接形容词或名词,如turn out / satisfactory (结果令人满意)、turn out a success (结果很成功)。

● It **turns out** that the office isn't relocating to Atlanta after all.

结果公司还是没有搬到亚特兰大。

听力小测验

Listening Comprehension

Listen to the conversation and answer the following questions.

1. a. ☐ Billy's hard work.

   b. ☐ Billy's job performance.

   c. ☐ Billy's sales.

2. a. ☐ For not working overtime and complaining.

   b. ☐ For using company time for personal matters.

   c. ☐ For having a motorcycle instead of a car.

3. a. ☐ Billy is late for work.

   b. ☐ The company is suing Billy.

   c. ☐ Billy's boss is very satisfied.

4. a. ☐ The man.

   b. ☐ The man's secretary.

   c. ☐ Billy himself.

欢迎新员工
WELCOMING A NEW EMPLOYEE

常见的 **6** 种甜点种类

美国人的零食有很多是小麦制品，且口味以甜的居多，常见的有以下几种：

❶ doughnut：又作donut，也就是"甜甜圈"，常裹上糖粉后，再撒上肉桂粉提味。

❷ pretzel：一种扭成条状的咸脆饼，上面撒芝麻，这是殖民地时代由欧洲传入美国的食品。

❸ bagel：一种硬的面包圈饼，有人译为"百吉饼"，这是犹太人的食物，但在美国常佐以果酱。

❹ muffin：一种烤成杯状的小松糕。口味可分甜咸两种，不过甜的变化较多，也常配卡布奇诺咖啡（cappuccino）或红茶（black tea）食用。

❺ pancake：一种圆形的松饼，常在上面淋蜂蜜（honey）或枫糖浆（maple syrup），再配上一杯鲜奶，当作早餐食用。

❻ chips：一种"炸马铃薯条"，是将马铃薯切成薄片，油炸沥油（烘干）后，再撒上盐制成。

对话范例 DIALOGUE

It is Toni Bradley's first day at Sun Tech. She arrives early and meets Jake Lancer by the door.

Jake: Good morning. You must be new here.

Toni: Is it that obvious?[1]

Jake: You're arriving with the **early birds**. We're part of an elite[2] few.

Toni: My name's Toni. Today is my first day.

Jake: I'm Jake. Pleased to meet you. You must be **filling** Brian's **shoes**.

Toni: That's right. Brian is training me all week, and then I'm **on** my **own**.

Jake: I'm just down the hall from you guys. There's a staff lounge[3] down there at the end of the hall.

Toni: Great.

Jake: There's a microwave and a coffee machine there. It's good to hang out in when the pressure[4] gets to be too much.

Toni: Thanks for the tip![5]

Jake: Well, see you later. Welcome aboard and good luck on your first day.

Toni: Thanks! I just might need it!

---

1. obvious [`ɑbvɪəs] *adj.* 明显的
2. elite [ɪ`lit] *n.* 精英
3. lounge [laʊndʒ] *n.* 休息室
4. pressure [`prɛʃɚ] *n.* 压力
5. tip [tɪp] *n.* 提示；劝告

中文翻译

托妮·布莱德利第一天到太阳科技上班。她很早就到了,在门口遇见了杰克·兰瑟。

Jake:	早安。你一定是新人。
Toni:	有那么明显吗?
Jake:	你到得很早。我们是少数的精英。
Toni:	我叫托妮,今天是我第一天上班。
Jake:	我叫杰克。很高兴认识你。你一定是来接布莱恩的位置。
Toni:	没错。布莱恩这个星期都会培训我,然后我就得靠自己了。
Jake:	我就在你们走道过去的另一头。走廊尽头有个员工休息室。
Toni:	太棒了。
Jake:	那边有微波炉和咖啡机。压力太大的时候,那是个轻松一下的好地方。
Toni:	谢谢你的建议!
Jake:	好了,待会儿见。欢迎加入,祝你第一天上班好运。
Toni:	谢谢!我也许正需要好运气!

学习重点

early bird 早起的人；早到的人

有句英文俗语说 The early bird catches the worm，表示
"早起的鸟儿有虫吃"，所以 early bird 就引申指"早起的人；早
到的人"，而 arrive with the early birds 则是指"早到"。

● A: You know what they say about **the early bird
    catching the worm**.

    你知道大家都说"早起的鸟儿有虫吃"吧。

   B: Yeah. I knew I should have hit this sale
    yesterday. All the good stuff is gone!

    对啊，昨天打折时我应该就来买。现在好货都没了！

fill (someone's) shoes 接替（某人的）位置

这是个比喻的说法，并不是真的去穿某人的鞋。shoes 在此是指
某人的"职位；职责"，此语表示"接替（某人的）位置或职位；
取代（某人的）角色"。

● I would hate to have to **fill** Steve's **shoes**! He was so
  efficient in his job.

  我绝不想接替史蒂夫的工作！他做事太有效率了。

on (one's) own 靠自己

这是个常见的用语，类似的说法为 by (oneself)。

● You're **on** your **own** here. I have no experience in
  this kind of situation.

  这你就要靠自己了。我对这种情况毫无经验。

Listening Comprehension

Listen to the conversation and answer the following questions.

1. *a.* ☐ Because she is often late.

   b. ☐ Because she is arriving early.

   c. ☐ Because she's under pressure.

2. *a.* ☐ Jake.

   b. ☐ Brian.

   c. ☐ Sally.

3. *a.* ☐ There are lots of pretty pictures hanging on the wall.

   b. ☐ Workers are allowed to keep their shoes in the lounge.

   c. ☐ It's a good place to get away to when the pressure builds.

4. *a.* ☐ A microwave and a coffee machine.

   b. ☐ A coffee machine and a water cooler.

   c. ☐ A microwave and a water cooler.

新进员工——
基本培训

TRAINING A NEW EMPLOYEE—
THE BASICS

秘书的工作

近年来,秘书(secretary)常改称为个人助理(personal assistant),其工作内容通常包括记录(keep records)、处理往来信函(correspondence)、协调安排小型及大型会议(coordinate meetings and conferences)、安排出差事宜(make travel arrangement),以及处理信件、电话和访客(screen mail, calls and visitors)等。随着商业竞争日趋激烈,国际化脚步更加快速,秘书的工作也越来越繁重。尤其是老板一天的行程(schedule)常要依靠秘书来安排或调整,如何依照优先原则(priority)来安排以避免时间冲突或错失重要会议,可就依赖于秘书的经验、对老板习惯的了解以及临场的应变。通常,良好的记忆力和有条不紊的组织力,是秘书必备的条件。

DIALOGUE

Brian Albertson is training Toni in her new job as Jake's assistant.

Brian: Good morning, Toni! I'm glad you're early. So, are you ready to be my **shadow**?

Toni: You bet. You **call the shots**. I'm right behind you.

Brian: OK. Here's the drill.[1] First, you'll check Jake's box in the mail room,[2] his voice mail, his e-mail, and his schedule for the day.

Toni: So I've really got to be on top of his schedule.

Brian: More than that, you've got to know his schedule **inside out** because he'll call by nine a.m. for the lowdown.[3]

Toni:	Call me?
Brian:	Yes, he's usually out the door and on the way to his first appointment by eight thirty a.m.
Toni:	Wow. How does he handle it?
Brian:	You. You're his home base.[4] Stay **on** your **toes** because sometimes Jake might have a surprise that he needs you to handle.
Toni:	Well, like they say: variety[5] is the spice of life.
Brian:	That's a good attitude[6] to have. There's never a dull[7] moment on the job. Before you know it, Friday will be here.
Toni:	Great! Well, this sounds like it's going to be an exciting challenge.

1. drill [drɪl] *n.* 演练；练习
2. mail room [`mel ˌrum] 邮件收发室
3. lowdown [`loˌdaʊn] *n.* 实情；内幕
4. home base [`hom `bes] 总部；根据地；本垒
5. variety [vəˈraɪətɪ] *n.* 变化；多样性
6. attitude [`ætəˌtjud] *n.* 心态；态度
7. dull [dʌl] *adj.* 枯燥无聊的

中文翻译   TRANSLATION

布莱恩·艾伯森正在培训新来的托妮成为杰克的新助理。

Brian: 托妮，早上好！很高兴你来得很早。那，你准备好接替我的位置了吗？

Toni: 当然。你发号施令吧，我会紧跟上你的。

Brian: 好，开始演练吧。首先，你要去收发室检查杰克的信箱、语音信箱、电子邮件，还有查看他今天的行程表。

Toni: 所以我真的得要完全掌握他的行程。

Brian: 不止这样，你还要彻底知道他的行程，因为他早上九点前会打电话问你详细情形。

Toni: 打电话给我？

Brian: 对，通常他八点半前就会出门赴第一场约会。

Toni: 啊，他怎么应付得来？

Brian: 靠你啦。你是他的总部。你得机灵一点，因为有时候杰克会有些突发的事情要靠你处理。

Toni: 嗯，大家都说：有变化，生活才会多姿多彩。

Brian: 这是很好的心态。这份工作不会有无聊的时候。不知不觉地，星期五就到了。

Toni: 太棒了！听起来这似乎会是个很刺激的挑战。

学习重点

shadow 接替者

shadow原指"影子"，在工作上，是指接受即将离职者的指导与培训的"接替者"；亦可作动词用，意思是"接替某人的位子"。

● I was elected as the next director, and I'll have the chance to **shadow** the current director before he leaves. I'll be his **shadow**.

我被选为下任总监，而且我将会有机会在现任总监离职之前接受他的培训。我将会接替他的位置。

call the shots 发号施令

也可说call the tune，表示"控制全局；发号施令"。

● The boss is usually the one who **calls the shots** for the company.

老板通常是公司里发号施令的人。

inside out 完全地；彻底地

此语原指"里面朝外"，也就是由"里里外外"之意，引申为"完全地；彻底地"。

● Mark knows the downtown district **inside out**.

马克对于市区了如指掌。

on (one's) toes 机警

直译为"踮起脚尖走路"，引申为"保持警戒；机警"。

● You need to be **on** your **toes** for any emergency.

你得随时警觉，以防紧急事件发生。

Listening Comprehension

Listen to the conversation and answer the following questions.

1. a. ☐ The man.
   b. ☐ Toni.
   c. ☐ Unknown.

2. a. ☐ Check Jake's box in the mail room.
   b. ☐ Clean Jake's office.
   c. ☐ Review Jake's report.

3. a. ☐ To get a hot cup of coffee.
   b. ☐ To get his mail.
   c. ☐ To get the lowdown on his schedule.

4. a. ☐ By eight thirty a.m.
   b. ☐ By eight thirty p.m.
   c. ☐ By nine a.m.

新进员工——
具体培训

TRAINING A NEW EMPLOYEE—
SPECIFIC DUTIES

各式各样的商展

trade show 是指"贸易商展",通常是在一个大型的贸易中心 (trade center) 里举行。每个公司通常会租下自己的摊位 (booth),以展示最新的产品或举办促销特卖 (promotional sales)。

另外,还有一种叫 fair,表示"市集"或"农业商展"。该项展览多以评选作物或牲畜来吸引参观者,如牛类展 (cattle show) 或农产品展览 (farm products exhibit),进一步达到促销农产品的目的。经评审评级后,一等奖可获蓝缎带奖 (blue ribbon);二等奖为红缎带奖 (red ribbon);三等奖则为黄缎带奖 (yellow ribbon),以作为奖励与确立品质保证的标准。

而另一种规模更大的 exposition 则为"博览会",简称为 expo。通常这属于国际性质的盛会,例如:每年在德国北部工业城市汉诺威 (Hannover) 举行的 CeBIT 电脑展,每年各国的电子相关产业都有不少厂商参加,也借此吸引了不少外资与订单,进而提升了"参与品牌"的知名度。

Brian continues to train Toni in her new job as Jake's assistant.

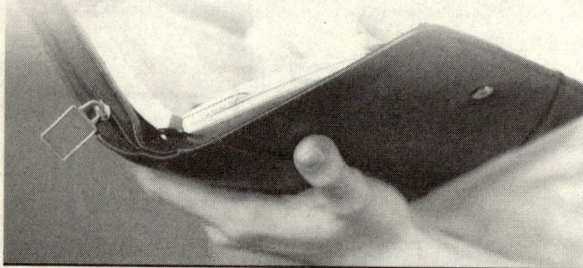

Brian: Around ten, the phones slow down a bit.

Toni: Oh, good. I understand I'm also responsible for human resources[1] in this department. What does that entail,[2] exactly?

Brian: Last-minute emergencies[3]—you know, like staff needing **sick leave** or the occasional[4] **temp** that needs to be called in.[5]

Toni: OK, I can handle that.

Brian: And then, of course, there's the regular list of things to do, like scheduling trade shows, organizing **in-house** meetings, and keeping the supply room stocked.

Toni: I think I should write all this down.

Brian: Oh, don't worry, you'll remember it all in no time. Oh, I almost forgot: you also need to approve staff overtime.

Toni: OK. And who approves my overtime? It sounds like I may need it in the beginning.

Brian: You **write** your **own ticket**. The general managers eventually see everything that you approve.

Toni: Wow! It sounds like this assistant might need an assistant.

Brian: You're going to do fine. This job just seems tough on the onset.[6]

---

1. human resources [ˈhjumən rɪˈsorsɪz] 人力资源
2. entail [ɪnˈtel] v. 必需；使承担
3. emergency [ɪˈmɜdʒənsɪ] n. 紧急情况
4. occasional [əˈkeʒənḷ] adj. 偶尔的
5. call in [ˈkɔl ˈɪn] 简短拜访
6. onset [ˈɑnˌsɛt] n. 开始

布莱恩继续培训托妮成为杰克的助理。

Brian: 十点左右，电话会稍微少一点。

Toni: 太好了。我知道我也必须负责本部门人力资源的调配。那到底需要做些什么？

Brian: 临时的突发状况——你知道的，像是有人请病假，或是偶尔需要请临时雇员等等。

Toni: 好的，那我应付得来。

Brian: 然后当然还有一些固定的工作，例如：安排商展日期、安排公司内部会议和补充办公室用品库存。

Toni: 我想我应该把这些都写下来。

Brian: 哦，别担心，你用不了多久就会全部记住的。哦，我差点忘了，你还得批准员工的加班单。

Toni: 没问题。那谁来批准我的加班单？听起来刚开始的时候，我可能会需要加班。

Brian: 你自己批。最后总经理会审查你批准的每件事。

Toni: 啊！听起来我这个助理好像还需要一位助手。

Brian: 你会做得很好的。这份工作只是刚开始看起来有点难而已。

学习重点

sick leave 病假

leave是"休假；准假"之意，其他常见的假有leave of absence（事假）、maternity leave（产假）、annual leave（年假）等。

● I heard Marge is on **sick leave**. I hope she gets well soon.

我听说玛姬生病请假。我希望她早日康复。

temp 临时雇员

temp是temporary的简称，指"临时的人、事、物"。在此是指temporary worker/employee（临时雇员）。

● While in college, I used to work as a **temp** for a **temp** agency.

大学时，我在一家临时工作中介公司当过临时工。

in-house（公司）内部的

反义词为out of the office/company（公司外的）。

● This week's meeting is **in-house**. Next week's meeting is at the Wells Corporation.

这星期的会议是在公司内部召开。下星期的会议是在威尔斯公司。

write (one's) own ticket（某人）自己决定

指某人可以依自己的判断或喜好来自由行事。

● We wanted him to work with us on the project so badly, that we let him **write** his **own ticket**.

我们非常想让他和我们合作进行这项计划，为此我们允许他按照自己的方法做事。

听力小测验 **GIVE IT A TRY!**

Listening Comprehension

Listen to the conversation and answer the following questions.

1. *a.* ☐ The secretary.
   b. ☐ The general managers.
   c. ☐ Human resources.

2. *a.* ☐ Around nine.
   b. ☐ Around eleven.
   c. ☐ Around ten.

3. *a.* ☐ Buying train tickets for the managers.
   b. ☐ Calling in the occasional temp.
   c. ☐ Taking care of staff needing sick leave.

4. *a.* ☐ Staff overtime.
   b. ☐ Staff attendance.
   c. ☐ Office supplies.

筹备会议
PLANNING A MEETING

关于会议

一般说来，会议里会有一位主席（chairman），而且有详细的议程（agenda）。每一阶段讨论的议题称为issue。与会的来宾叫做attendant，而未能出席者则是absentee。

在讨论中，若有人对该项议题提出相反的论点（argument），则可能会出现争论（disputation），若争论不断持续下去，无法达成共识（agreement / consensus），主席通常会宣布休会（recession），做私下的协调沟通；或者将会议延期（adjournment），择期再议。

Jake talks to his new assistant Toni about setting up a meeting.

Jake: Toni, I need you to send out a memo by e-mail to announce[1] a meeting.

Toni: OK. Give me the details, and I'll send it out right away.

Jake: **Address** it **to** all staff in the marketing department. The meeting will be at two o'clock on Thursday the sixth, in the main **conference room** on the second floor.

Toni: But next Thursday is a **public holiday**. We don't work on that day.

Jake: I completely forgot. Thanks for reminding[2] me. Please change the meeting to Monday the tenth then.

Toni: The tenth? OK. And what is the purpose of that meeting?

Jake: I want us to discuss and evaluate[3] the marketing strategy for next year. Tell everyone I expect to see sales figures from each marketing sector.

Toni: Anything else, sir?

Jake: I'm also expecting to hear any ideas they have on alternative[4] marketing schemes.[5]

Toni: OK, I'll get right on it.

Jake: Oh, and one more thing. Tell everyone to be on time![6]

---

1. announce [əˈnaʊns] v. 宣布；发布
2. remind [rɪˈmaɪnd] v. 提醒
3. evaluate [ɪˈvæljuˌet] v. 评估
4. alternative [ɔlˈtɜnətɪv] adj. 替代性的；不同的
5. scheme [skim] n. 计划；方案
6. on time [ɑn ˈtaɪm] 准时

中文翻译   **TRANSLATION**

杰克吩咐他的新助理托妮安排一场会议。

Jake: 托妮，我要你用电子邮件寄出一份备忘录，作为开会通知。

Toni: 好的，请告诉我细节，我马上发出去。

Jake: 寄给所有营销部的员工。在本月6号，星期四下午两点，到二楼大会议室开会。

Toni: 但是下星期四是法定假日。那天我们不上班。

Jake: 我完全忘了。谢谢你提醒我。那请把日期改到10号星期一吧。

Toni: 10号？好的。那么会议的目的是什么？

Jake: 我要大家一起讨论并评估明年的营销策略。告诉大家我希望能看到每个营销区域的销售数据。

Toni: 还有吗，先生？

Jake: 我也希望能听到他们对其他的营销计划有什么想法。

Toni: 好，我会马上处理的。

Jake: 哦，还有一件事。告诉大家要准时到！

address (something) to (someone)
寄 (某物) 给 (某人)

address [əˈdrɛs] 作动词有许多意思，可以表示"在……写上收件人的姓名和地址"，例如：address (something) to (someone) 表示"寄 (某物) 给 (某人)"；也可以指"向 (某人) 演说；称呼"。address 作名词时还可读作 [ˈædrɛs]，表示"地址"，例如：e-mail address (电子邮件地址)。

● Please **address** this package **to** the director of accounting.

　请把这个包裹寄给会计室主任。

conference room 会议室

另一个常用的说法是 meeting room。

● Our **conference room** is fully equipped to handle any kind of presentation.

　我们的会议室设备齐全，做任何形式的简报都没问题。

public holiday 国家法定假日

public holiday 是指大家都不用上班上学的国家法定假日，也可称为 national holiday，但请不要和 national day (国庆日) 搞混了。

● Christmas is a **public holiday** in Western countries.

　圣诞节在西方国家是法定假日。

听力小测验　　　　　　　　　　　**GIVE IT A TRY!**

Listening Comprehension

Listen to the conversation and answer the following questions.

1. *a.* ☐ Send out an e-mail.
   b. ☐ Call all staff.
   c. ☐ Write a marketing report.

2. *a.* ☐ All staff in the marketing department.
   b. ☐ All staff in the sales department.
   c. ☐ All staff in the shipping department.

3. *a.* ☐ Thursday the sixth.
   b. ☐ Monday the tenth.
   c. ☐ Friday the fifth.

4. *a.* ☐ To discuss and evaluate the shipping strategy for next year.
   b. ☐ To discuss and evaluate the marketing strategy for next year.
   c. ☐ To discuss and evaluate the sales strategy for next year.

裁员
LAYING OFF WORKERS

被裁员后的**4**大心态调整建议

裁员的英文说法有很多种，包括 downsizing、streamlining、delayering、reduction in force、redundancy elimination 等等。经济不景气时，被遣散的员工该如何应对？

❶ 面对现实，并了解这不是你的错。这是公司管理层的组织过渡期，你无法做主。

❷ 积极主动。如果现在的工作并不是你的长期目标，正好趁此机会确立新的目标，做好规划。

❸ 保持乐观。别只看事情的负面而忽略了正面意义，遣散后也可能出现意想不到的转机。

❹ 自我推销。公司政策有重大改变时，正是欢迎建议和新想法的时候，可借此机会提出建设性的意见来推荐自己，也许可以借此加入到公司的企划行列（planning sessions）中。

To avoid going into bankruptcy,[1] Top Flight Airlines is downsizing. Paul Green, the company's president, is asking Adam West, the new vice president, for advice.

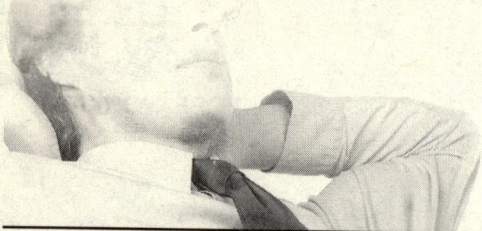

Paul: Adam! Do you have any suggestions on how we can avoid this bankruptcy?

Adam: Downsizing could reduce[2] our operating costs.

Paul: Where do you suggest **making** staff **cuts**?

Adam: The logical[3] place to start would be in administration.

Paul: That's not going to **go over** very well.

Adam: I know. But I think that if we computerize the office, we could reduce office staff by about twenty percent just by eliminating[4] a lot of the paper work.

Paul: OK. If we **lay off** twenty percent of the administrative staff, will that be enough to get the company **back on track**?

Adam: Unfortunately not. We will also need to make some cuts in the service department.

Paul: How can we do that and maintain the level of service that we offer our passengers?

Adam: Well, we'll have to retrain[5] the service staff and streamline[6] operations, so we won't need as many people to run things smoothly.

Paul: Well, this is serious, and I really don't think we have any other choice. If we keep losing money like this, we'll have to shut everything down.

---

1. bankruptcy [`bæŋkrəpsɪ] *n.* 破产
2. reduce [rɪ`djus] *v.* 减少；降低
3. logical [`lɑdʒɪkl] *adj.* 符合逻辑的；合理的
4. eliminate [ɪ`lɪmə͵net] *v.* 消除；排除
5. retrain [ri`tren] *v.* 重新培训；再培训
6. streamline [`strim͵laɪn] *v.* 简化（工作流程）而提高效率

为了避免破产，顶尖航空公司正准备缩编。公司总裁保罗·格林正在向新任副总裁亚当·威斯特征询意见。

Paul: 亚当！对于如何避免公司破产，你有没有什么建议？

Adam: 缩编可以降低我们的运营成本。

Paul: 你认为该裁掉哪个部门的员工？

Adam: 最合理的就是从行政部门开始裁。

Paul: 员工不会乐意接受的。

Adam: 我知道。不过我想如果我们让办公室电脑化，就能减少许多文书工作，也就能裁减20%的员工。

Paul: 好吧。如果我们裁掉20%的行政人员，那样足以让公司重新上轨道吗？

Adam: 很遗憾的是，并不能。我们还必须裁掉一部分的服务部人员。

Paul: 那样我们要如何维持对旅客的服务品质呢？

Adam: 我们必须重新训练服务人员并精简运营步骤以提高效率，这样一来不需要那么多人员就可顺利运营。

Paul: 嗯，这真的很严重，而且我实在不认为我们有别的选择。如果我们像这样一直赔钱的话，整家航空公司都得关闭。

学习重点

make cuts 缩减；裁减

此语常用来表示"减少浪费或多余的活动、消费、人力等"，如 make staff cuts（裁员）、make salary cuts（减薪）。

- Our company is having trouble maintaining profitability, so we have to **make** budget **cuts**.

  由于公司无法维持获利，所以我们必须删减预算。

go over 被接纳；给人某种印象

常与表达好坏的副词，如 well 或 badly 连用。how does (something) go over with (someone) 则是用来问"（某人）对（某事物）的接受度或反应如何"。

- They're pulling out of the deal? That won't **go over** well with the boss.

  他们不做这笔交易了？老板不会乐意接受这种情况的。

lay off 裁员；暂时解雇员工

这个短语表示"受到经济不景气影响而裁员或暂时解雇员工"。

- The car factory is shutting down this summer and expects to **lay off** around one thousand workers.

  今年夏天这家汽车工厂即将关闭，预计会解雇约 1 000 名员工。

back on track 重新上轨道

track [træk] 是指"轨道"。back on track 字面上是"回到正轨"，也就是"事情回到正常、顺利的状态"。

- After two quarters in the red, this company is **back on track**.

  这家公司在亏损了两个季度之后又重新上了轨道。

Listening Comprehension

Listen to the conversation and answer the following questions.

1. a. ☐ Downsizing.
   b. ☐ Hiring more people.
   c. ☐ Increasing operating costs.

2. a. ☐ Shutting down the office.
   b. ☐ Cleaning the office.
   c. ☐ Computerizing the office.

3. a. ☐ No, it's not enough.
   b. ☐ Yes, it's enough.
   c. ☐ It doesn't say.

4. a. ☐ People from administration and the marketing department.
   b. ☐ People from administration and the sales department.
   c. ☐ People from administration and the service department.

考虑换职业
CONSIDERING A CAREER CHANGE

公共关系

Public Relations (公关) 简称为PR，是指政府部门或商业机构，通过消息发布、举办活动等方式，与公众建立起良好互动的关系。例如：利用某种形象打造广告等，使民众对某个人物、想法、产品或机构产生兴趣，进而产生正面的大众印象 (favorable public opinion)。因此，就商业而言，越高的曝光率则表示商品的商机越大，潜在的销售量也会攀升。而政府所进行的公关通常较具政治意味，范围遍及海内外，通常称为propaganda (政治宣传)，常属于外交策略中的一种积极手法。

在口语中，美国人有时会称一个刚出校门的新人为PR nerd，指其在人际关系上可能表现得生涩、不够圆滑，又略带一丝紧张。nerd为俚语，通常指一个手脚笨拙、人际关系不佳或不擅长社交，甚至行为异常的人。而在电脑风行以后，则又用来指长时间沉浸于电脑所构筑的世界里，不知如何与人正常相处的"电脑痴"。

　　　　　　　　　　　　　　　DIALOGUE

Fran Glen works for Top Flight Airlines and is thinking about changing jobs. She is talking to a coworker, Craig Whitmore, about the possibilities.[1]

Fran:　　I've really got to think about my future. You've heard of the cutbacks[2] management's making, right?

Craig　　Come on, they won't let you go. You've been here too long. Besides, you enjoy your job.

Fran:　　That's true, but I feel like I've reached the **glass ceiling** in this company.

Craig　　Glass ceiling?

Fran:　　I've been working here for ten years. I haven't gotten a promotion in three years. I thought I'd be VP by now.

Craig: There's no official company policy, but it's true that they don't promote women to management positions here.

Fran: I think it's time to change jobs, and maybe even careers,[3] if I want to **get ahead**.

Craig: If you change careers, what will you do?

Fran: I'm doing market research here, but I studied public relations in college. I could do PR for a large multinational[4] company.

Craig: That sounds exciting, and the pay would be better, too. Yeah, if I were you, I would **keep an eye on** the job postings[5] on the Internet.

---

1. possibility [ˌpɑsəˈbɪlətɪ] n. 可能性
2. cutback [ˈkʌtˌbæk] n. 减少
3. career [kəˈrɪr] n. 生涯；事业
4. multinational [ˌmʌltɪˈnæʃən] adj. 跨国的
5. posting [ˈpostɪŋ] n. (网络上的) 帖子；公告

中文翻译　　　　　　　　　　　　　　　TRANSLATION

弗兰·格兰在顶尖航空工作，正在考虑要换工作。她正在和同事克雷格·惠特摩讨论换工作的可能。

Fran: 我真的必须思考一下我的未来。你听说了管理层最近打算裁员，对吧？

Craig: 拜托，他们不会裁掉你的。你是资深员工。而且，你喜欢这份工作。

Fran: 是没错，但是我觉得我在这家公司里已经遇到升职时的无形障碍了。

Craig: 无形的障碍？

Fran: 我在这里已经工作了10年。这3年来我都没有升职。我原以为我现在应该已经当上副总裁了。

Craig: 虽然公司没有明文规定，但是在这里女性无法升到管理层却是事实。

Fran: 我想是该换工作的时候了，如果我想超越目前的成就，或许甚至该换个职业。

Craig: 如果换职业，你想做什么？

Fran: 我在这里做的是市场研究，但是我在大学念的是公共关系。也许我可以到一家大型的跨国公司做公关。

Craig: 那听起来挺刺激的，而且待遇也会比较好。嗯，如果我是你，我会注意网上有什么招聘消息。

学习重点

glass ceiling 工作升职中无形的障碍

glass ceiling（玻璃天花板）是借玻璃透明、看不见，但仍造成阻碍的特性，引申用来指"在工作上因性别或种族歧视等因素而无法升到高级职位的不成文规则"。

● The company is known for its **glass ceiling**; they never promote women.

这家公司是以升职中的无形障碍而闻名；他们从来不让女性晋升。

get ahead 成功；进步；出人头地

用来指工作上、学业上等的"成功进步"，也就是超越目前的状况，向前迈进。

● What would you suggest I do to **get ahead** in this company?

你建议我该怎么做才能在这家公司有所晋升？

keep an eye on 紧盯着；留意

keep an eye on 这个惯用语字面上是指"把眼睛放在……上"，意思是"留意；专心看；仔细观察"，请注意这里 an eye 固定用单数形式。

● We need to **keep an eye on** our competition, or we will lose market share.

我们必须注意我们的竞争对手，不然我们的市场占有率就会下降。

听力小测验

Listening Comprehension

Listen to the conversation and answer the following questions.

1. *a.* ☐ Three years.
   b. ☐ Twelve years.
   c. ☐ Ten years.

2. *a.* ☐ Three years.
   b. ☐ Twelve years.
   c. ☐ Ten years.

3. *a.* ☐ Do PR for a multinational company.
   b. ☐ Do market research for a multinational company.
   c. ☐ Act as a become a VP for a multinational company.

4. *a.* ☐ Marketing.
   b. ☐ Public relations.
   c. ☐ Business administration.

避免罢工
AVOIDING A STRIKE

工会的产生

员工常为了要改善其经济地位 (economic status) 和工作环境 (working conditions / environment)，而组成一个团体，以集体为主体和雇主交涉 (bargain) 或甚至争论 (argue)，这就是"工会"的由来。

工会依其组织特性可分成两种：一种是horizontal / craft union，会员从事同一种手工艺或专业行业，如"木匠工会"；另一种则叫做vertical / industrial union，会员专业的领域不同，但从事或服务于同一种行业，如"汽车工会"。

工会除了争取劳动权益外，有时也扮演"环保先锋"的角色。因为随着环保意识的兴起，从事农业、化工业、电路板等重污染制造业的员工，也陆续在同事之间发现一些因污染引起的职业病或职业伤害，于是通过工会向公司争取改善工作环境、改良废料处理以达到排放标准等，除了保障员工良好的工作环境外，也促使雇用方努力达到环保的要求。

DIALOGUE

A few months after downsizing the airline, the employees of Top Flight Airlines are ready to **go on strike**. The leader of the workers' union, Joe Bradley, is talking to Adam West.

Adam: I've asked you to meet with me today to see if there is some way we can avoid a strike.

Joe: The employees are very unhappy. Unless some significant[1] changes are made, we plan to go on strike Monday and **picket** in front of the airport to protest the low pay and poor working conditions.

Adam: I believe we can come to a compromise[2] on some of your demands.[3]

Joe: OK, specifically which demands?

Adam: You want a six-percent pay increase **across the board**. We'd be willing to give you three percent.

Joe: The employees will not accept an increase of only three percent.

Adam: We'd be willing to give three percent now and an additional[4] one percent in six months.

Joe: If you would do that and reduce the working hours from nine to eight hours a day, I will present your proposal[5] to the union.

Adam: I'll do that right away. We really hope to avert a strike.

Joe: Yes. A strike would be costly[6] for everyone.

---

1. significant [sɪg`nɪfəkənt] 重大的
2. compromise [`kɑmprəˌmaɪz] 和解；妥协
3. demand [dɪ`mænd] 要求；请求
4. additional [ə`dɪʃənl] 另外的；附加的
5. proposal [prə`pozl] 计划；提案
6. costly [`kɔstlɪ] 昂贵的

中文翻译　　　　　　　　　　　　　　　　TRANSLATION

在公司裁员几个月后，顶尖航空的员工们准备要罢工。工会领导
乔·布莱德利正在和亚当·威斯特谈话。

Adam:　我请你今天和我碰个面，是想看看有没有什么办法可
以避免罢工。

Joe:　员工们非常不高兴。除非公司做出一些重大的改变，
否则我们将在星期一进行罢工，并在机场前布置罢工
纠察队，以抗议低薪和恶劣的工作环境。

Adam:　我相信公司对你们所提出的某些要求可以做出妥协。

Joe:　好吧，可否确切指出是哪些要求？

Adam:　你们要求全面加薪6%。公司愿意给你们加薪3%。

Joe:　只加3%员工们不会接受的。

Adam:　公司愿意现在加3%，6个月后再加1%。

Joe:　如果你们愿意那么做，并把工作时间从一天9小时减
到8小时，我会把你的提案呈报给工会。

Adam:　我会立刻去办。公司真的希望能避免罢工。

Joe:　是啊。罢工对每个人来说都要付出很大的代价。

学习重点

go on strike 进行罢工

在进行罢工 (go/be on strike) 之前，通常会展开谈判 (talks)，如果雇佣双方各让一步 (make concessions)，或许可以达成共识 (come to an agreement) 而避免 (avoid/avert) 罢工，不然谈判破裂 (break off talks) 后，结局可就难以预料了，但是可以确定的是，双方都得付出代价。

● If they don't make concessions by noon, the workers vow to **go on strike**.

如果他们中午之前还不肯让步，工人们发誓要进行罢工。

picket 布置罢工纠察队

picket [`pɪkɪt] v. 布置罢工纠察队；n. 罢工纠察员

罢工通常都是由工会 (union) 所发起，在国外常会设置罢工纠察，一般是在公司或者工厂的重要出入口进行抗议，让每天来上班的人都得先通过罢工纠察队所筑起的人墙 (cross the picket line) 才能进公司上班，目的是希望公司能早日与工会进行对话，进而达成协议。

● There were many protesters **picketing** outside the White House.

有许多抗议者在白宫外围布置了罢工纠察队。

across the board 全体的；全面的

本短语原本是指赌马时把赌注下在告示板上列举的所有热门马匹上以提高中奖机会，引申指"全面性的"。

● I expect all of our product lines to increase five percent **across the board** this year.

我期望今年我们所有的产品线都能全面增产5%。

听力小测验　　　　　　　　　　　　　　　**GIVE IT A TRY!**

Listening Comprehension

Listen to the conversation and answer the following questions.

1. a. ☐ Because of the low pay and long hours.
   b. ☐ Because of the terrible supervisors.
   c. ☐ Because of the unfair promotions.

2. a. ☐ Six percent.
   b. ☐ Three percent.
   c. ☐ One percent.

3. a. ☐ The company can meet all of the workers' demands.
   b. ☐ The company is willing to discuss the workers' demands.
   c. ☐ The company doesn't wast to do anything right away.

4. a. ☐ Eight hours.
   b. ☐ Nine hours.
   c. ☐ One hour.

宣告破产
DECLARING BANKRUPTCY

宣告破产

当一家公司的销售收入 (sales revenue) 无法达到财务计划 (financial plan) 所订立的目标时, 称为收入上的不利差异 (earning lags behind estimates)。当这种情况日趋严重时, 可能就得解雇 (lay off) 员工。至于被遣散的员工, 或者说是非自愿性失业 (involuntary disembarking) 的人, 只好另谋出路。如果公司一直找不出方法来让业绩达到预定的目标, 甚至也找不到方法来筹措或募集资金 (raise capital), 经过一段时间后, 其负债 (in debt) 超出了清偿能力时, 也就只能申请破产 (file for bankruptcy), 把公司的所有权 (ownership)、设备 (facilities) 交给法院来处理清算债务 (liquidation)。之后, 法院再指派破产管理人 (trustee in bankruptcy) 来处理其债权人 (debtee /obligee) 如何分配赔偿金 (dividend) 的相关事宜。

Compton Tech, a competitor of Sun Tech's, is in
trouble. Here, the company's CEO, Gina Thomas,
talks to a manager, Tom Franklin, about declaring
bankruptcy.

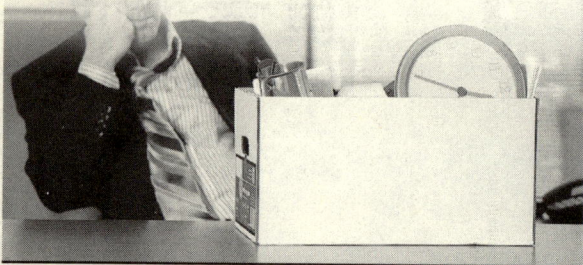

Gina: Come in! Hi. Have a seat. I'm afraid I have
some very bad news.

Tom What is it?

Gina: Well, the company has been experiencing
serious financial difficulty for quite some
time now.

Tom Yeah. I know we've been operating **in the
red** for the past few months.

Gina: Exactly. And after a lengthy[1] discussion
with the board of directors,[2] I've come
to the conclusion that the best course of
action[3] is to file bankruptcy.

Tom: Bankruptcy!? I didn't know we were in such serious financial trouble.

Gina: Sales have been low all year long, and with Sun Tech and Digicom discussing a merger, I feel the situation wouldn't turn around[4] for another year. We simply can't afford to **keep our doors open** that long.

Tom: When do you plan to make the announcement[5] to all the employees?

Gina: Early next week.

Tom: What kind of **severance package** will we be able to offer them?

Gina: Unfortunately, the best we can do is offer one month's salary.

Tom: Oh! How terrible!

---

1. lengthy [`lɛŋθɪ] *adj.* 冗长的
2. board of directors [`bɔrd əv də`rɛktəz] 董事会
3. course of action [`kɔrs əv `ækʃən] 行动方针
4. turn around [ˌtɜn ə`raund] 反转；完全改变
5. announcement [ə`naunsmənt] *n.* 宣布；公告

中文翻译　　　　　　　　　　　　　　　TRANSLATION

太阳科技的竞争对手之一康普顿科技正面临危机。该公司的CEO 吉娜·托马斯正在和一位经理汤姆·弗兰克林讲到即将宣布破产 的事。

Gina: 进来！嗨，请坐。我恐怕有很坏的消息要告诉你。

Tom: 怎么了？

Gina: 嗯，公司在财务上陷入困境已经有一阵子了。

Tom: 嗯。我知道过去几个月来公司一直是赤字。

Gina: 确实如此。经过一次冗长的董事会议之后，我的结论 是：最好的做法就是宣布破产。

Tom: 破产！？我不知道我们的财务问题有这么严重。

Gina: 我们整年的销售状况一直都很差，而且太阳科技和数 码通信正在讨论合并，我认为再过一年公司情况也不 会好转。我们实在没办法撑那么久。

Tom: 你打算什么时候向所有员工宣布？

Gina: 下星期周初吧。

Tom: 我们能够提供什么样的遣散条件？

Gina: 很不幸地，我们最多只能多发1个月的薪水。

Tom: 哦！真是太糟糕了！

学习重点

---

in the red 赤字的；亏损的

red 在此指"赤字"，in the red 的意思是"亏损的"；相反短语为 in the black（获利的）。

- Our company was **in the red** all year.

  我们公司这一整年来都处于亏损状态。

---

keep our doors open 继续运营

这是比喻的用法，直译为"保持公司大门敞开"，表示"继续运营"的意思。

- To **keep our doors open**, we had to take a loan from the bank.

  为了要继续运营，我们必须要向银行贷款。

---

severance package 遣散方案

severance [ˈsɛvərəns] *n.* 解除契约；解雇

遣散方案是保障员工离开公司时能得到应得的利益，通常是指 severance pay（遣散费），但也可能包含其他福利，如优惠保险费、协助寻找新工作等等。

- When Fred was fired, he received a **severance package** from the company.

  弗雷德被开除后得到了公司遣散方案的保障。

听力小测验　　　　　　　　　　　　　　**GIVE IT A TRY!**

Listening Comprehension

Listen to the conversation and answer the following questions.

1. a. ☐ The company is going to downsize.
   b. ☐ The company is going to strike.
   c. ☐ The company is going to file bankruptcy.

2. a. ☐ Sun Tech and Compton Tech.
   b. ☐ Compton Tech and Digicom.
   c. ☐ Sun Tech and Digicom.

3. a. ☐ Later next week.
   b. ☐ Early next week.
   c. ☐ Two weeks later.

4. a. ☐ Serious financial difficulty.
   b. ☐ Serious human resources shortage.
   c. ☐ Serious computer incidents.

产品营销
MARKETING A PRODUCT

广告类型

一般广告可分为两大类：平面媒体的纸质广告宣传
（advertisement）以及广播电视、电子媒体的多媒体广告
（multimedia commercial）。

平面媒体一般是指报纸（newspaper）和杂志（maga-
zine），除了在上面刊登广告外，还可以利用目录
（catalog）、海报（poster）、传单（flyer）、公路广告展
板（signpost）等来达到效果；而广播电视、电子媒体
则包括电视（television）、广播（radio）和新兴的网络
（Internet）。其中，电视因为属于强势媒体，是单向直
接把影像传输给观众，一般也认为效果最好又最直接，因
此广告费用最高。而广播则以即时、密度高与价廉的特
性，受到区域性厂商的欢迎。

但是，随着网络的风行，电子化的商务广告颇有后起之秀
的态势，不过就整体而言，目前还不成气候，倒是未来的
发展值得注意。而网络上部分网页里含有的广告，通常是
横跨网页的长条状的，称为banner ads，较接近于平面媒
体的宣传方式。

DIALOGUE

Sam Palmer is speaking at a training seminar[1] about the marketing plans for the year. Chris Weeks and Lora Paine, new members of the sales team, have several questions.

Sam: It is important that we understand the merchandise[2] we're marketing.

Chris: **What if** we think a product is inferior?[3]

Sam: Good question. In that case, you should write a report. In our company, we **strive for** quality.

Chris: What if we find problems with some of the merchandise?

Sam: Again, if you discover a flaw,⁴ you should write a report. It's the only way we can do anything about it.

Lora: It's good to know that our company **stands behind** their products.

Sam: We do. Now, about this year's marketing scheme, we are launching a major advertising campaign in August.

Lora: What kind of advertising will we be using?

Sam: Radio and print.

Chris: Do we get to preview⁵ some of this or . . . ?

Sam: I thought you'd never ask. All the details of the upcoming campaign are outlined in this plan. Let's have a look.

---

1. seminar [ˈsɛmə‚nɑr] *n.* 研讨会
2. merchandise [ˈmɜtʃən‚daɪz] *n.* 商品
3. inferior [ɪnˈfɪrɪə] *adj.* 较差的；劣等的
4. flaw [flɔ] *n.* 瑕疵；缺点
5. preview [ˈpri‚vju] *v.* 预览

中文翻译 　　　　　　　　　　　　　　TRANSLATION

山姆·帕姆尔正在培训研讨会上讲到今年的营销计划。两位新业务员克里斯·威克斯和洛拉·潘恩有几个问题要问。

Sam:　　了解我们营销的商品是很重要的。

Chris:　　如果我们觉得某项产品品质比较差怎么办？

Sam:　　问得好。如果是那样的话，你应该写一份报告。我们公司总是致力于提升产品的品质。

Chris:　　如果我们发现有些商品有问题，该怎么办？

Sam:　　同样的，如果你发现瑕疵，也该写份报告。只有这样我们才能设法改进。

Lora:　　知道公司会为产品负责，真是不错。

Sam:　　是的。那，关于今年的营销策略，我们将在8月举办一个重要的广告活动。

Lora:　　我们会用哪一类型的广告？

Sam:　　广播和平面广告。

Chris:　　我们可以先看其中一部分，或者……？

Sam:　　我还以为你们不会问呢。近期所有宣传活动的细节都列在这个方案里。我们来看看吧。

学习重点

what if 如果……怎么办

what if是what would happen if（如果……怎么办）的省略形式，后面接从句。另外，what if也可用来表示提议，表示"如果……如何"。

- **What if** everything goes wrong?

  如果事情出差错，怎么办？

strive for 致力于

strive for (something) 表示"尽全力完成（某事），力求做到最好"。

- We always **strive for** excellence.

  我们总是努力做到最好。

stand behind 支持

此语字面意思是"站在……后面"，引申表示"支持"，也可以说back up。

- I will **stand behind** you and your decision.

  我会支持你和你的决定。

GIVE IT A TRY!

Listening Comprehension

Listen to the conversation and answer the following questions.

1. *a.* ☐ Write a report.
   b. ☐ File a complaint.
   c. ☐ Return the product.

2. *a.* ☐ Meeting the deadline.
   b. ☐ Writing a report.
   c. ☐ Understanding the merchandise.

3. *a.* ☐ The company stands behind their products.
   b. ☐ The company's products are inferior.
   c. ☐ The company doesn't care about quality.

4. *a.* ☐ Launch a major advertising campaign.
   b. ☐ Go on strike immediately.
   c. ☐ Try to shut down the company.

增加媒体
曝光率
INCREASING MEDIA EXPOSURE

电子商务

电子商务（e-commerce）指的就是网上交易（on-line transactions），主要可分为公司对客户（business-to-customer, B2C）和公司对公司（business-to-business, B2B）两大类。

一般说来，前者指顾客在网上，通过门户网站（portal site）的介绍，选定产品后，采用信用卡（credit card）付费的交易模式，客户较不固定，交易金额不大，以量取胜，如网络书店 Amazon.com、网络拍卖店 eBay，或是网上的股票交易等等。

后者则为上下游产业伙伴、同行之间的大批交易，因为生意金额庞大，品质为重，安全性要求更高。新兴的虚拟私有网络（VPN, virtual private network）即为达此目的而开发出的技术，让企业双方在 Internet 的公共网络上，架构出既安全又具私密性的通道，为 B2B 的发展打下基础。

Sam is talking with Sally, his assistant. They are discussing ways to promote their products.

Sally: Mr. Palmer, I have some ideas on how we can successfully promote the new line.

Sam: I'm always **open to** any good **suggestions**.

Sally: Well, I was thinking that traditional forms of advertising, like radio, television, magazine ads, newspaper ads, might not be the best way to **get** our customers' **attention**.

Sam: Billboard[1] advertisements are a good way.

Sally: True. But I think there is a way that we can get an even greater number of customers.

Sam: Sounds like this might be expensive. You know we have a limited[2] advertising budget for this product.

Sally: What would you say if I told you we could increase public exposure[3] at a lower advertising cost than our proposed[4] budget?

Sam: I'd say great. Now, quit **beating around the bush**. What **have** you **got in mind**?

Sally: Advertising on the Internet.

Sam: The Internet?

Sally: Of course! We just set up our own Web site, link it up[5] to related sites, and make it possible for customers to order online.

Sam: Sally, you are brilliant!

---

1. billboard [ˈbɪlˌbɔrd] n. 露天大型广告牌
2. limited [ˈlɪmɪtɪd] adj. 有限的；被限制的
3. exposure [ɪkˈspoʒɚ] n. 曝光
4. proposed [prəˈpozd] adj. 计划好的；所提议的
5. link up [ˈlɪŋk ˌʌp] 连接；连线

中文翻译　　　　　　　　　　　　　　TRANSLATION

山姆正在和他的助理莎莉谈话。他们在讨论促销产品的方式。

Sally: 帕姆尔先生，对于如何成功促销公司新的产品线，我有一些想法。

Sam: 任何好意见我都愿意接受。

Sally: 嗯，我一直在想，传统的广告手法，例如：在广播、电视、杂志和报纸上做广告，未必是吸引客户注意力的最好方法。

Sam: 用广告展板是一个不错的方法。

Sally: 没错。不过我认为还有一个方法能够吸引更多的顾客。

Sam: 听起来好像会花很多钱。你知道，我们这个产品的广告预算很有限。

Sally: 如果我告诉你，我们可以用比原先所做的预算更少的广告费，让产品得到更高的公众曝光率，你觉得如何？

Sam: 当然是好极了。好了，别兜圈子了，你有什么想法？

Sally: 在网络上登广告。

Sam: 网络？

Sally: 当然！我们建设自己的网站，和相关网站连接，并且让顾客可以在网络上直接订购。

Sam: 莎莉，你真聪明！

学习重点

open to suggestions 欢迎任何建议

表示自己愿意多听别人的意见，鼓励别人有建议就提出来。

● I don't have any plans this afternoon, but I am **open to suggestions**.

我今天下午没有任何计划，不过欢迎你提出建议。

get (someone's) attention 吸引（某人的）注意

attention [ə`tɛnʃən] *n.* 注意

其他类似的说法还有 attract / capture / catch (someone's) attention。

● We need to **get** the public's **attention** with this advertising.

我们要用这则广告吸引大众的注意力。

beat around the bush 兜圈子；拐弯抹角

bush [buʃ] 原指"灌木丛"，引申为"问题或事情的核心"。beat around the bush 表示"兜圈子；拐弯抹角"，而口语中常用否定形式来要求别人有话直说。

● Get straight to the point when you talk to the boss. He doesn't like people to **beat around the bush**.

跟老板说话时要直接说重点，他不喜欢别人说话兜圈子。

have (got) in mind 内心的想法是

what have you got in mind 常用来问别人"心里在想什么；有什么想法"。

● I heard you are making plans for the summer. What **have** you **got in mind**?

我听说你在为暑假作计划。你有什么想法？

Listening Comprehension

Listen to the conversation and answer the following questions.

1. a. ☐ Radio, the Internet, and magazine ads.
   b. ☐ Television, newspaper ads, and the Internet.
   c. ☐ Radio, television, and magazine ads.

2. a. ☐ Newspaper ads.
   b. ☐ The Internet.
   c. ☐ Billboard advertisements.

3. a. ☐ A limited budget.
   b. ☐ An unlimited budget.
   c. ☐ A huge budget.

4. a. ☐ It increases public exposure and advertising costs.
   b. ☐ It lowers public exposure and advertising costs.
   c. ☐ It increases public exposure and lowers advertising costs.

商务简报

DELIVERING A BUSINESS PRESENTATION

会议相关用语

一般会议的目的不外乎是为了讨论一项方案 (proposal)，或是探讨一项计划 (project)，大多会先由主管进行简报 (briefing)，或是提出成果预计报告 (presentation)，再针对特定议题 (issue) 来讨论。

而一般会议的设备与用具包括讲台 (podium)、麦克风 (microphone)、白板 (whiteboard)、投影仪 (overhead projector)、幻灯机 (slide projector) 以及图表 (graph / chart / diagram and table) 等。

Josie Gleason has been with Sun Tech for two years. Recently, she was promoted to assistant sales manager. Today, she is giving a presentation to Jake Lancer, the sales manager, regarding next year's sales.

Josie: Please take a look at these **comparison charts**. They illustrate[1] the sales generated[2] in this region over the past five years. As you can see, there hasn't been much growth.

Jake: Yes. Sales are strong, but they should be stronger. And individual[3] product sales?

Josie: The products out of Mexico are doing very well, while those from Thailand are not.

Jake: Is this due to[4] poor quality or the price?

Josie: Neither. It has to do with design. Five of the six designs out of Mexico City were created from customer feedback.[5]

Jake: What are you **getting at**, Josie?

Josie: Nobody knows the customer better than Sales, so I propose that we organize **cooperative teams** with the sales and design departments to create next year's product line.

Jake: Terrific idea, and I'm sure the others will agree. Glad to have sharp[6] people like you on the team, Josie.

Josie: Thanks, Jake.

---

1. illustrate [`ɪləstret] v. (用图、实例等) 说明
2. generate [`dʒɛnəˌret] v. 产生
3. individual [ˌɪndəˈvɪdʒuəl] adj. 个别的；单独的
4. due to [`djuˈtu] 由于
5. feedback [`fidˌbæk] n. 反映；反响
6. sharp [ʃɑrp] adj. 精明的；机灵的

中文翻译   TRANSLATION

乔西·格利森已经在太阳科技工作两年了。最近她被升为销售部经理助理。今天，她正在向销售部经理杰克·兰瑟做有关明年业务的简报。

Josie: 请看一下这些对照图表。这些图表显示出过去5年来这个地区的业绩。你可以看出业绩并没有多大的增长。

Jake: 是啊，虽然销售业绩不错，但应该还可以更好。个别产品的销售业绩如何？

Josie: 墨西哥制造的产品卖得很好，而在泰国制造的则不然。

Jake: 是因为品质不佳，还是价格的问题？

Josie: 都不是。是设计的关系。墨西哥厂的产品中，6件里有5件是根据客户回函的建议进行设计的。

Jake: 乔西，你的意思是？

Josie: 没有人比销售部更了解顾客，所以我建议我们让销售部门与设计部门组成联合团队来设计明年的产品线。

Jake: 非常棒的构想，我确定其他人都会同意的。乔西，很高兴我们团队中有像你这么精明的人。

Josie: 谢谢你，杰克。

学习重点

comparison chart 对照图表

comparison [kəm`pærəsn̩] *n.* 比较；对照
chart [tʃɑrt] *n.* 图表；曲线图

商业简报中，常会运用到一些统计或比较对照的图表，例如：销售业绩、年度业绩增长趋势，或单一商品在不同区域的销售情况等，这是因为图表通常比文字更让人一目了然。

● These **comparison charts** indicate a ten-percent growth in sales, doubling our growth from last year.

这些对比图表显示出我们的销售业绩增长了 10%，是去年增长率的两倍。

get at 暗指；意指

get at 有许多不同的意思，例如："到达；触及；挖苦；贿赂"等，在此是用来表示没有直接讲出来，但是间接所指，也就是"暗示；意指"的意思。

● So you want to start the project over? Is that what you're **getting at**?

那么你希望整个计划重新来过吗？你的意思是这样吗？

cooperative team 合作团队

这是指"跨部门的合作团队"。当公司遇上了大项目或为了保持竞争力，时常会成立这样的团队，整合相关的资源，以求在商场上立足。

● The members of the **cooperative** medical **team** come from both Europe and Asia.

这个医疗合作团队的成员来自于欧洲以及亚洲。

听力小测验   **GIVE IT A TRY!**

Listening Comprehension

Listen to the conversation and answer the following questions.

1. *a.* ☐ There's something wrong with the design.

   b. ☐ There's something wrong with the price.

   c. ☐ There's something wrong with the quality.

2. *a.* ☐ The products out of Mexico.

   b. ☐ The products out of the USA.

   c. ☐ The products out of China.

3. *a.* ☐ Making the sales and design departments cooperate.

   b. ☐ Lowering the price of the products from Mexico.

   c. ☐ Increasing the number of salespeople in Thailand.

4. *a.* ☐ He thinks it's a bad idea.

   b. ☐ He thinks it's a terrific idea.

   c. ☐ He thinks it's a useless idea.

审核预算案
REVIEWING A BUDGET PROPOSAL

会计年度

一个会计年度（fiscal / financial year）的开始，也就是开始结算账户、计算赋税（tax）的时候。各国的会计年度有所不同，美国的会计年度从10月开始；而一般国家的会计年度则与公历年（calendar year，自1月1日至12月31日）一样，是从1月起算。

想要了解一家公司的运营状况，可以从资产负债表（balance sheet）、年周转率（annual turnover rate）等数据来获得信息。简单地说，公司的总营业额（total sales revenue）减去各项成本（costs）与运营支出（expenditures / expenses）后，可得到收入（income）。如果收入达到收支平衡点（breakeven），表示收入刚好足以支付所有的成本；超过则有盈余或利润（profits），否则，未达标准出现负值，就是亏损或赤字（deficit）了。

对话范例   DIALOGUE

Jake is meeting with Ned Williams to discuss the budget proposal[1] for the next fiscal year.

Ned: Jake, I understand you've completed the budget proposal for the next fiscal year. I'd like to go over that with you.

Jake: I just happen to have it with me.

Ned: Great. What does it include?

Jake: It covers all **operating costs**. And I've **broken** them **down** into categories.

Ned: Ah, I see, projected costs for overhead,[2] sales and administrative expenses, materials, advertising, production, and R & D.

Jake: That's correct. Each one is then broken down further into subcategories.[3]

Ned: What about insurance costs?

Jake: That **falls under** overhead.

Ned: Unfortunately, these figures are five percent over budget.

Jake: Yes, I'm aware of that. It's all based on our current operating costs and then adjusted for next year's inflation.[4]

Ned: Well, this definitely calls for some budget cuts[5] because, above all, we need to maintain our profitability.[6] Let's see if the staff have any suggestions on what to cut first.

Jake: Good idea, sir.

---

1. proposal [prə`pozl] *n.* 计划；方案
2. overhead [`ovəˌhɛd] *n.* (企业等的) 经常性支出
3. subcategory [sʌb`kætəˌgorɪ] *n.* 细目
4. inflation [ɪn`fleʃən] *n.* 通货膨胀
5. budget cut [`bʌdʒɪt ˌkʌt] 缩减预算
6. profitability [ˌprɑfɪtə`bɪlətɪ] *n.* 收益性；收益率

中文翻译　　　　　　　　　　　　　　TRANSLATION

杰克正在和奈德·威廉姆斯开会讨论下个会计年度的预算计划。

Ned:　杰克，我知道你已经完成下个会计年度的预算企划书。我想和你一起审核。

Jake:　我刚好带在身上。

Ned:　太好了。预算包括了哪些项目？

Jake:　包括了所有的运营费用。我已经将它们分成几个类别。

Ned:　哦，我知道了，你把预算分成了经常性支出、营销与行政费用、原料费、广告费、生产成本和研发成本。

Jake:　没错。然后每个类别都又再分成更细的细目。

Ned:　那保险费用呢？

Jake:　那个列在经常性支出中。

Ned:　可惜，这些数字比预算高出了5%。

Jake:　是的，这我知道。这些都是根据我们目前的运营成本，再依明年的通货膨胀调整过的。

Ned:　嗯，这样一定得删减一些预算，因为最重要的是我们必须维持获利。我们先看看员工对于要先削减哪一部分的预算有没有什么建议。

Jake:　好主意，先生。

学习重点

operating costs 运营成本

经营公司所需的成本，如机器设备费、人事费、交通费等。

● Our **operating costs** for next year will reflect this year's efforts to cut back.

公司今年裁减预算的效应会在明年的营业成本上显现出来。

break (something) down 将（某事物）细分

break表示"打破；打碎"，因此break (something) down是指"把（某事物）细分成更小的部分"。另外，break down也可以用来指"（机器）故障；（系统）失灵"等意思。

● The task list for this committee still needs to be **broken down** into sections.

委员会的职务表还需要再细化成几个项目。

fall under 归到……下面；属于……范围

fall under在此并不是指"掉到……底下"，而是指某事物"归到……下面；隶属于……"。

● Anything related to design **falls under** the art department.

任何与设计相关的事情都归美术部管。

　　　　　　　　　GIVE IT A TRY!

Listening Comprehension
Listen to the conversation and answer the following questions.

1. a. ☐ The budget proposal for the next fiscal year.
   b. ☐ A business presentation.
   c. ☐ A severance package.

2. a. ☐ All operating costs.
   b. ☐ Human resources costs.
   c. ☐ Profitability.

3. a. ☐ Advertising costs.
   b. ☐ Overhead expenses.
   c. ☐ Production costs.

4. a. ☐ Three.
   b. ☐ Six.
   c. ☐ Five.

股票上市
INITIAL PUBLIC OFFERING

什么是NASDAQ?

只要是涉足股票投资的人应该都知道美国的NASDAQ，它是National Association of Securities Dealers Automated Quotation System的缩略语。这是一个自动报价的股票电脑系统，每天报出超过 5 000 支股价，其中多以高科技产业股为主。

而要成为NASDAQ的会员，公司需有相当的资本与实力，以在小型资本市场（Small Cap Market）首次上市的公司为例，需要有 5 000 万美元的市场资本（capital）或 400 万美元的资产（assets）、100 万股的公开发售股（public shares）和 300 名以上的股东（shareholders）等条件。

Ned Williams, the company's president, is talking to Jake and Josie about the company's **going public**.

Ned: You know, this has been a privately-owned company since we first opened in 1975, and, to be honest with you, I'm **inclined to** keep it that way.

Jake: But the market is changing rapidly. We need to think long-term and **take** proactive[1] **measures**, otherwise we will find ourselves behind the competition.

Ned: That's a good point. Perhaps I should be more open-minded[2] about this.

Josie: I agree with Jake. We simply can't afford to upgrade our facilities without considerable outside investment. The bank will not loan us **that kind of money**.

Jake: Even if it did, the interest rate[3] on that much capital[4] would be more than we can afford. I'm convinced the only way to generate the funds we need is to go public.

Josie: A consultant[5] will be coming in next week to explain the registration procedure for an IPO.

Ned: That's great because I want everyone to have a thorough understanding of what this entails before any decisions are made.

Josie: Of course. We all need to think this through.[6]

---

1. proactive [pro`æktɪv] *adj.* 预先的；未雨绸缪的
2. open-minded [ˌopən`maɪndɪd] *adj.* 开明的；无偏见的
3. interest rate [`ɪntərɪst ˌret] 利率
4. capital [`kæpətl] *n.* 资本；资金
5. consultant [kən`sʌltənt] *n.* 顾问
6. think through [`θɪŋk`θru] 彻底想清楚

中文翻译

公司总裁奈德·威廉姆斯正在和杰克以及乔西讨论公司股票公开上市的事。

Ned: 你们知道,从1975年开始运营以来,本公司就一直是私人经营,老实说,我比较倾向于保持现状。

Jake: 但是市场瞬息万变,我们必须要做长远打算,未雨绸缪采取行动,否则就会落后给竞争对手。

Ned: 你说得很有道理。也许对这件事我应该更开明一点。

Josie: 我同意杰克所说的话。如果不对外募集大量的资金,我们根本负担不起升级设备的费用。银行可不会借我们那么大笔的贷款。

Jake: 就算银行肯,公司也负担不起这么一大笔资金的利息。我相信要筹到我们需要的资金,唯一的办法就是股票上市。

Josie: 下个星期会有一位顾问来向您解释股票上市的注册程序。

Ned: 很好,在做出任何决定之前,我要大家对股票上市所涉及的事有全盘的了解。

Josie: 当然。我们大家都应该要彻底地想清楚。

学习重点

go public 股票公开上市

go public 是"股票公开上市"的口语说法，而 initial public offering 则为正式用法，作名词用，通常简称 IPO。

● Our company **went public** last year.

我们公司的股票去年公开上市了。

inclined to 倾向于

inclined 这个形容词表示"倾斜的"，而 inclined to 用来形容人则表示"（性格上）倾向于；赞成……"。

● I am more **inclined to** support the tax cut.

我个人赞成减税。

take measures 采取措施

measure 表示"措施；手段"，常为复数形式，如 extreme measures（激烈手段）、preventive measures（防范措施）。

● If the power doesn't come back on soon, we're going to have to **take** drastic **measures** to keep these shipments cold.

如果电力没有很快恢复，我们就必须做出紧急应对措施使货品保持冷冻。

that kind of money 那么一大笔钱

that kind of money 不能直译成"那种钱"，而是表示金额大得惊人，也就是"那么大的数目；那么一大笔钱"。

● Where did you get **that kind of money**? I thought our account was empty!

你从哪里弄到那么多钱的？我以为我们的账户已经空了！

听力小测验　GIVE IT A TRY!

Listening Comprehension

Listen to the conversation and answer the following questions.

1. a. ☐ 1977.
   b. ☐ 1975.
   c. ☐ 1976.

2. a. ☐ Think long-term and take proactive measures.
   b. ☐ Think short-term and take proactive measures.
   c. ☐ Think long-term and take no action.

3. a. ☐ Upgrade the facilities.
   b. ☐ Be open-minded.
   c. ☐ Loan money.

4. a. ☐ File bankruptcy.
   b. ☐ Go public.
   c. ☐ Sell the company.

讨论议题
DISCUSSING AN ISSUE

会议讨论

开会时针对某些重要议题（issues）发言的人，我们称之为主要发言人（keynote speaker），如果发言人讲的话很有建设性（constructive），或者甚至提出了创新的（innovative）理念或想法，往往可以得到许多正面的回应（positive feedback），或许还能让整个会议流程加速完成。

但事情可能不如预期，当与会人士讨论陷入僵局（deadlock）而僵持不下时，往往需要动用到高层决策者（higher-up decision maker）出面，来做最后的决策。

通常在谈判时，面对面接触（face-to-face／direct contact）是很重要的，除了可以化解一些不必要的误解外，沟通起来也比较顺畅，如果能找出一个双赢方案（win-win solution），借此让双方都受益（benefits for both sides），那么问题就很容易解决了。

Ned is meeting with Sun Tech's managers to discuss production and where to make cuts in the future.

Sam: Can we afford to continue carrying older models, **given the fact that** their technology is inferior to the rest of our lines?

Ned: OK, Sam, in your opinion, what is the **worst-case scenario** if we continue as we are?

Sam: Sales on the older models are down. If our orders go below the minimum,[1] production costs will **shoot through the roof**. I propose we cut costs now, before we take a loss.

Jake: But we have customers who are very satisfied with the systems they've been using over the past few years. We should at least continue to stock service items.

Kelly: I'm with Jake. The clientele[2] that have been with us the longest are a valuable asset to the company.

Jake: I agree. If we insist on changing our clients' systems every time something new comes along,[3] we run the risk of losing them forever.

Sam: But we do have an obligation[4] to keep them up on the latest innovations.[5]

Ned: OK. I think it is premature[6] to discontinue anything at this point. Let's continue to explore our options.

---

1. minimum [`mɪnəməm] n. 最小量；最低限度
2. clientele [ˌklaɪənˈtɛl] n. (统称) 顾客；常客；老主顾
3. come along [`kʌm əˈlɔŋ] 发生；出现
4. obligation [ˌɑbləˈgeʃən] n. 义务；责任
5. innovation [ˌɪnəˈveʃən] n. 新发明；创新
6. premature [ˌpriməˈtjʊr] adj. 过早的；匆忙的

中文翻译   TRANSLATION

奈德正在和太阳科技的经理们开会讨论生产制造以及未来该如何缩减成本的问题。

Sam: 考虑到老产品的科技比我们其他线的产品差，我们还能继续销售老产品吗？

Ned: 好吧，山姆，依你看，如果公司照目前这样继续下去，最坏的情况会是怎样？

Sam: 老产品的销售量在下降。如果公司订单低于最低量，生产成本就会急速上涨。我建议公司现在就停止生产，以免以后亏损。

Jake: 但我们有些客户对过去几年来使用的这些系统非常满意。我们至少应该继续保留一些维修品的库存。

Kelly: 我同意杰克的话。长期使用公司产品的老主顾是公司宝贵的资产。

Jake: 我同意。如果公司坚持一有新产品推出，就改变客户的产品系统，我们会存在永远失去这些客户的风险。

Sam: 但是我们有义务让客户跟上最新技术。

Ned: 好吧。我想现在谈论停止生产任何东西都还太早。我们来继续探讨别的选择。

学习重点

given (the fact) that 考虑到……

given 在此当介词或连接词用，意思是"考虑到……"，也可用 considering 来替代。

● **Given the fact that** she's never worked in accounting before, I don't think we should hire her.

考虑到她先前从未做过会计，我认为我们不该聘用她。

worst-case scenario 预计的最坏状况

scenario [sɪˋnɛrɪo] 原本指"剧本"，在此指"预计未来事情发展的情况；想象情况"，因此 worst-case scenario 指的是"设想中最坏的情况"，而相反词则是 best-case scenario（预想中最好的情况）。

● In the **worst-case scenario**, we could have to start all over again.

最坏的情况是，我们有可能必须再重新开始。

shoot through the roof 急速攀升

roof 是"屋顶"，引申为"极限、顶点"的意思。shoot through the roof 直译为"冲破顶点"，表示物价等"迅速往上攀升"。另外有一个短语 go through the roof 则表示某人"大发雷霆"，请不要混淆。

● The price of fuel **shot through the roof** after the Gulf War.

海湾战争后，油价便急速攀升。

听力小测验 GIVE IT A TRY!

Listening Comprehension

Listen to the conversation and answer the following questions.

1. a. ☐ Production costs will shoot through the roof.
   b. ☐ Production costs will go down quickly.
   c. ☐ Production costs will stay the same.

2. a. ☐ Reduce the production costs.
   b. ☐ Develop new products.
   c. ☐ Stock service items.

3. a. ☐ New customers.
   b. ☐ Their current clientele.
   c. ☐ The office buildings.

4. a. ☐ They might lose these clients forever.
   b. ☐ The number of customers might increase.
   c. ☐ The production costs might go down.

达成决议
RESOLVING AN ISSUE

签约

在商场上，签约对双方来说都是一件重要的事。通常双方都先会针对某些议题来做全面性的探讨，经过评估（evaluation）或协商（negotiation）后，找出解决之道（solution），就可以说双方已达成共识（come to a consensus、arrive at an agreement）。而在融洽气氛之下，则很可能会打铁趁热，随即签下合约（signing of a contract）。合约通常是对方对等互惠的双边协议（bilateral agreement）；另外，还有只利于单方的单边协议（unilateral agreement）。至于国与国之间达成共识，所签下的书面文件，则称为条约（accord、treaty 或 pact）。

DIALOGUE

Sun Tech's president and managers have been discussing production problems and are now coming to an agreement on the best solutions.

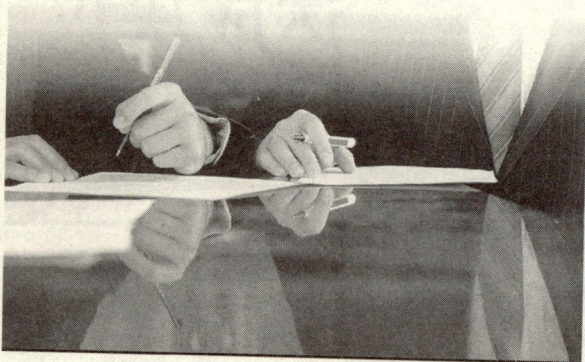

Ned: Jake, which models of our older series[1] are our best sellers?[2]

Jake: **Off the top of** my **head**, the Original Series' 98, the Portable, and the Mega Series are the most popular.

Ned: How many older systems can we reasonably continue **for the sake of** service?

Sam: Right now we have ten. If we could phase out[3] seven or eight of them, our profits would nearly double.

Kelly: Wow! It really is expensive to run smaller productions, isn't it?

Sam: That's what I've been **saying all along**.

Jake: And on the whole, the overall[4] quality of our stock will increase and help bring in[5] steadier[6] profits.

Sam: Then there's our answer.

Ned: I believe we all agree that for now, we can select three of the older series to carry as complete systems. We'll phase out all others with our next catalog and carry service items for everything.

Jake: Sounds good.

Sam: Suits me fine.

Kelly: I'm with you.

---

1. series [`sɪrɪz] *n.* 系列
2. best seller [`bɛst`sɛlə] 畅销货品
3. phase out [`fez `aut] 逐步去除；渐渐废止
4. overall [`ovəˌɔl] *adj.* 全部的；全面的
5. bring in [ˌbrɪŋ `ɪn] 产生或带来（利润、收入等）
6. steady [`stɛdɪ] *adj.* 稳定的；持续的

中文翻译

太阳科技的总裁和经理们一直在讨论生产问题，现已达成共识，想出了最好的解决之道。

Ned: 杰克，公司以往系列的商品哪几项最畅销？

Jake: 在我记忆中，原先的98系列、手提系列以及Mega系列是最受欢迎的。

Ned: 如果为了服务客户的话，我们能合理地保留几个以前的系列？

Sam: 目前我们有10个系列。如果我们能逐步淘汰掉七八个，利润几乎可增至两倍。

Kelly: 啊！小量生产的成本真高，不是吗？

Sam: 那正是我一直强调的重点。

Jake: 而且整体来说，所有存货的品质都将有所提升，有助于带来更稳定的获利。

Sam: 那么这就是我们的答案了。

Ned: 我相信大家都同意目前我们该从以往系列产品中挑选三项来继续全面生产。在下次的目录上，我们会逐步删除其他的项目，并准备好所有商品的维修库存。

Jake: 听起来不错。

Sam: 我觉得很适合。

Kelly: 我同意你的说法。

学习重点

off the top of (one's) head
不经考虑；就（某人）记忆而言

off the top of (one's) head是口语用法，表示"未经考虑就回答"，也就是没有严谨地查询资料，随口说出，引申表示"就（某人）记忆而言"。

- A: How much money have we spent this year on supplies?

  我们今年在日常用品上花了多少钱？

  B: Right **off the top of my head**, I would say about ten thousand.

  在我记忆中，我想大概是1万元左右。

for the sake of (something) 为了（某事）

sake是指"理由；缘故"，for the sake of (something) 表示"为了（某事）的缘故；因为（某事）"，类似于because of (something)。

- **For the sake of** tradition, let's not cancel the Christmas party.

  基于传统，我们就不要取消圣诞舞会了吧。

say all along 一直强调

I have been saying all along表示"我一直强调"、"我早就说过了"。所以在需要把自己一贯的想法再说一遍时，便可用这句话加重语气。

- I've been **saying all along** that our service isn't good enough.

  我一直在强调我们的服务做得还不够好。

Listening Comprehension

Listen to the conversation and answer the following questions.

1. a. ☐ The Original Series 98.
   b. ☐ The Portable.
   c. ☐ The Multi Series.

2. a. ☐ Twelve.
   b. ☐ Ten.
   c. ☐ Eight.

3. a. ☐ Their profits would go down.
   b. ☐ Their profits would nearly double.
   c. ☐ Their profits would stay the same.

4. a. ☐ The overall quality of their stock would increase.
   b. ☐ It would help bring in steadier profits.
   c. ☐ They would attract even more customers.

讨论有可能的兼并

DISCUSSING A POSSIBLE MERGER

公司合并前的评估

无论是要并购（merger）或与另一家公司合资经营
（joint venture），都得要先了解对方的虚实才行。而要
了解一家公司的运营状况，莫过于要详细地评估管理团队
（management team）的运作和审核财务报告（financial
reports）。前者指的是人事（personnel），特别是销售
团队（marketing and sales team）、公司成员的阵容组合
（office support）以及技术支持（technical support）
这三部分；后者则是指盈利分析（profit analysis），通常
是通过一些报表，分析一家公司的销售额（sales）、工资
（salaries）、管理费用（overhead）、净利润（net profit）
与未来获利预测等等。经过了以上两关的考查，再考虑应
不应该合并，才比较妥当。

对话范例　　　　　　　　　　　　　DIALOGUE

Sun Tech has called a meeting with all managers to discuss a possible merger[1] with Digicom, its competitor. During a break, Jake Lancer and Kelly Moss discuss **the pros and cons** of such a merger.

Jake: You know, I think the merger is an excellent idea.

Kelly: That's true. However, I don't think this is the best time to think about expanding[2] operations.

Jake: Why not?

Kelly: The global recession[3] has been causing worldwide instability.[4] I think we should continue concentrating on the domestic market since we've been so successful here.

Jake: But Digicom is a well-known company.

Kelly: According to the **financial reports** they gave us, their profits have taken a nosedive[5] over the last two years.

Jake: Most international companies have taken a loss recently.

Kelly: That's exactly my point. I think we should wait. We have a responsibility to our stockholders[6] to increase company profitability and stock values.

Jake: But I think the benefits far outweigh[7] the risks in this case.

Kelly: Well, we'll find out how the others feel when we **put** the issue **to a vote**.

---

1. merger [`mɜdʒə] *n.* 合并
2. expand [ɪk`spænd] *v.* 扩增；扩展
3. recession [rɪ`sɛʃən] *n.* (经济) 不景气
4. instability [ˌɪnstə`bɪlətɪ] *n.* 不稳定；不稳固
5. nosedive [`nozˌdaɪv] *n.* 暴跌
6. stockholder [`stɑkˌholdə] *n.* 股东
7. outweigh [aʊt`we] *v.* 比……重要；胜过……

中文翻译　　　　　　　　　　　　　TRANSLATION

太阳科技召集所有经理开会讨论有可能和竞争对手数码通信合并的议题。在中间休息时，杰克·兰瑟和凯利·摩斯在讨论合并的优缺点。

Jake: 你知道，我认为合并是个非常好的主意。

Kelly: 的确如此。不过，我不认为现在是扩大运营规模的最佳时机。

Jake: 为什么不是呢？

Kelly: 全球性的经济不景气造成世界各地经济不稳定。我认为既然我们在这里做得这么成功，就应该继续专注于国内市场。

Jake: 但是数码通信是一家非常知名的公司。

Kelly: 根据他们提供的财务报表，过去这两年他们的获利大幅衰退。

Jake: 大部分的跨国公司最近都有亏损。

Kelly: 那正是我的重点，我觉得公司应该要等一等。我们有责任增加公司获利及股价，以对持股人负责。

Jake: 但是我认为这个项目的利益比风险多得多。

Kelly: 嗯，当这个提案进行表决时，我们就会知道其他人是怎么想的。

学习重点

the pros and cons (of something)
（某事物的）优缺点

pros是指advantages（优点），cons是指disadvantages（缺点），所以也可说成the advantages and disadvantages（of something）。

● We should think carefully about **the pros and cons** of this deal.

我们应该仔细考虑一下这桩交易的利弊得失。

financial report 财务报表

财务报表又称financial statement，详细地记录了公司各种经济活动。就以资产负债表（balance sheet）为例，其中包括了以下5个主要项目：流动资产（liquid asset）、固定资产（fixed asset）、流动负债（liquid liabilities）、长期负债（long-term liabilities）和股东益（stockholders' equity）。

● That company seems strong and stable. However, their **financial report** shows otherwise.

那家公司似乎健全稳固，然而从他们的财务报表看来却不是这么一回事。

put (something) to a vote 将（某事）付诸表决

vote是指"表决"。在会议中，投票者（voter）常以选票（ballot）或举手（show of hands）的方式进行表决。

● The issue of closing the factory will be **put to a vote** this Thursday.

关闭工厂的这项议题将在本周四付诸表决。

听力小测验　　　　　　　　　　　GIVE IT A TRY!

Listening Comprehension

Listen to the conversation and answer the following questions.

1. a. ☐ Companies filing bankruptcy.

   b. ☐ High inflation.

   c. ☐ The global recession.

2. a. ☐ Because they've been successful with it.

   b. ☐ Because they don't want to lose local customers.

   c. ☐ Because they don't have much money.

3. a. ☐ They have taken a loss.

   b. ☐ They have gone bankrupt.

   c. ☐ They have expanded operations.

4. a. ☐ The benefits far outweigh the risks.

   b. ☐ The profits are incalculable.

   c. ☐ The risks far outweigh the benefits.

写企划书
WRITING A BUSINESS PROPOSAL

一般商业书信分为 **6** 部分

❶ 标题（heading）：包括寄件人住址（return address）和日期（date），写在最上方。

❷ 收件人住址（inside address）：包括收件人的姓名（name）、称谓（title）、公司（company）或机构（organization）、地址（address）等。

❸ 称呼语（salutation）：包括向对方致意和问候的话。

❹ 正文（body）

❺ 文末敬语（complimentary close）

❻ 签名（signature）

对话范例 DIALOGUE

Jake and Kelly have been asked to **polish up** a business proposal for a joint venture[1] between Sun Tech and Digicom.

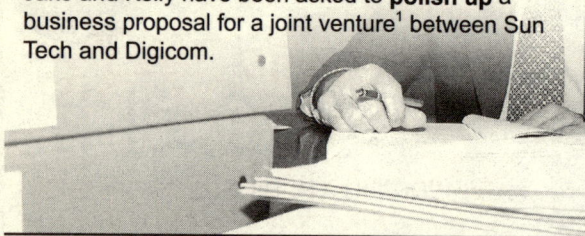

Jake: OK. We should clarify the wording[2] in the last paragraph and take into consideration the suggestions that Digicom gave.

Kelly: Right! And I think the introduction **comes across as** being too strong.

Jake: We could strike[3] it, and just **go straight into** the terms of the proposal.

Kelly: No, I say we modify it. The intro is good for introducing the key points of the proposal. What about the financial terms?

Jake: In the last negotiation, a sixty-forty profit share in Sun Tech's favor was proposed, but we don't know if Digicom is truly satisfied with the outcome.[4]

Kelly: Well, let's stick with those figures and see if they counter[5] the offer.

Jake: Let's also beef up[6] this part regarding **stock options** and public exposure—you know, accentuate[7] the positive.

Kelly: You're pretty slick,[8] Jake. That's a good idea. And when does this need to be submitted?[9]

Jake: ASAP. Should they not accept it as is,[10] we need to give ourselves a little time buffer.[11]

Kelly: OK. Then as soon as we're finished here today, I'll send it to the lawyer.

Jake: Great!

---

1. joint venture [ˌdʒɔɪnt `vɛntʃə] 合资企业
2. wording [`wɜdɪŋ] n. 措辞；说法
3. strike [straɪk] v. 删除；取消
4. outcome [`autˌkʌm] n. 结果
5. counter [`kauntə] v. 反对；对抗
6. beef up [`bif `ʌp] 改进；加强
7. accentuate [æk`sɛntʃuˌet] v. 强调；突显
8. slick [slɪk] adj. 聪明的；机智的
9. submit [səb`mɪt] v. 提交；呈递
10. as is [`æz ˌɪz] 按原状
11. time buffer [`taɪm ˌbʌfə] 缓冲时间

中文翻译　　　　　　　　　　TRANSLATION

杰克和凯利受命改进一份太阳科技和数码通信合资的企划书。

Jake: 好，我们应该把最后一段的措辞阐释清楚，并将数码通信的建议列入考虑范畴。

Kelly: 没错！我认为前言这样写会显得太过强势。

Jake: 我们可以删掉这段，直接提出企划案的条件。

Kelly: 不，我想修改一下就可以了。前言可以介绍企划案的重点。那有关财务的条款呢？

Jake: 在上一次的协商中，我们提议以6：4的比例来分配利润，太阳科技分得较多，但是我们不知道数码通信对这样的结果是否真的感到满意。

Kelly: 我们就坚持这个比率，看看他们反不反对。

Jake: 我们也要加强有关认股权以及公众曝光率的这部分——你知道，要突显好的一面。

Kelly: 杰克，你真是精明。那是个好主意。这份企划书什么时候要送出去？

Jake: 愈快愈好。万一他们不接受这份企划案，我们需要给自己一点缓冲的时间。

Kelly: 好吧。那只要我们今天一完成，我就把它寄给律师。

Jake: 很好！

学习重点

polish up 修饰；润饰

polish [`pɑlɪʃ] v. 磨光；擦亮

polish up 原指"磨光；擦亮（某物）"，引申为"修饰；改进"之意，亦可用来表示"温习；复习"某事物。

● You need to **polish up** your French skills.
你的法语能力需要提升。

come across as 给人某种印象；令人感觉

come across as 后面可接名词或形容词，表示"给人某种印象或感觉；看起来像是……"。

● He often **comes across as** arrogant.
他常常让人觉得他很傲慢。

go straight into 直接进入到

表示省掉一切的客套或排场，不说闲话，直接进入主题。西方人通常喜欢这种直接的表达方式。

● Let's **go straight into** the first item in our meeting.
我们直接进入会议的第一个讨论事项吧。

stock option 股票认购权

公司常会提供员工股票认购权，让员工可以成为公司的小股东，以加强员工对公司的参与感和凝聚力。

● That company offered **stock options** to many of its employees.
那家公司给许多员工提供股票认购权。

Listening Comprehension

Listen to the conversation and answer the following questions.

1. a. ☐ The wording in the last paragraph.
   b. ☐ The suggestions from Digicom.
   c. ☐ The way profits are shared.

2. a. ☐ The wording in the last paragraph.
   b. ☐ The suggestions that Digicom provided.
   c. ☐ The out come of the last meeting.

3. a. ☐ Seventy-thirty.
   b. ☐ Sixty-forty.
   c. ☐ Eighty-twenty.

4. a. ☐ Stock options and profit share.
   b. ☐ Public exposure and profit share.
   c. ☐ Stock options and public exposure.

庆功宴
CELEBRATION

员工奖励

如果某些员工表现优异而使公司业绩增长，公司通常会在公司大会（company convention）召开时，奖励这些表现优异的员工。有些公司则采抽取佣金（commission）或由公司分发红利奖金（bonus）等方式。再者，如果该员工的能力足以承担更多的责任，公司通常会给予升职（promotion），让他或她有一个更宽广可挥洒的空间，说起来，这何尝不是另一种加薪（raise、boost in pay）的方式呢？

另一方面，公司如果能多为员工的需求设想，在工作环境、休息时间与弹性工作等方面考虑周详，常能收到意想不到的效果。例如：在办公室另开设一间用餐室，并提供微波炉等设备，让部分员工可以自行携带午餐来享用，还能借此促进同事间的情谊，合作起来也就顺畅多了。因此，要是有适当的规划与设想，这样的效果可能更胜于发奖金。

DIALOGUE

Sun Tech has far surpassed[1] their sales goals in the last year, and they are hosting[2] a party for the company and its associates.[3]

Ned: Well, if I can have your attention, please. Thanks to all of you, we've had a very successful year. Before we get things under way,[4] Jake Lancer, sales manager, and Kelly Moss, marketing manager, have something that they'd like to share with us.

Jake: Good evening, everyone. **First off**, we would like to thank you for taking the time to give us your feedback and **constructive criticism** on the designs of the new lines.

Kelly: With your feedback, we went **back to the drawing board**, and the results were a smashing[5] success.

Jake: Thanks to everyone here tonight, Sun Tech has become the leader in the industry.

Kelly: And because of our success, Sun Tech and Digicom, the leader in digital telecommunications, will be working in partnership next year towards a brand new line.

Jake: That's right. Our goal is to **take** telecommunications **to the next level**.

Kelly: If you think this year was great, wait till next.

Ned: OK, OK. Thanks you two and thanks to everyone. On that note, let's get this party rolling.[6]

---

1. surpass [sə`pæs] v. 胜过；优于
2. host [host] v. 主办
3. associate [ə`soʃɪɪt] n. 伙伴；同事
4. under way [`ʌndə `we] 开始进行的；进行中的
5. smashing [`smæʃɪŋ] adj. （口语）极好的；非凡的
6. get (something) rolling [`gɛt `sʌmθɪŋ `rolɪŋ]
   开始进行（某事）

中文翻译

太阳科技的销售业绩已经远远超过去年订的营业目标,他们现在正为公司和员工同仁举办庆功宴。

Ned: 嘿,请大家注意这边。多亏了各位的努力,我们今年成果丰硕。在我们开始之前,销售部经理杰克·兰瑟和营销部经理凯利·摩斯有些话要和我们分享。

Jake: 大家晚安。首先,我们要感谢大家花时间为新产品线的设计提供了回馈意见和建设性的批评建议。

Kelly: 基于你们反馈的建议,我们将产品重新设计,结果空前成功。

Jake: 感谢今晚在场的各位,太阳科技已经成为这一行的龙头。

Kelly: 因为我们的成功,从明年起,太阳科技将会和数码通信界的领导厂商数码通信合作,一同开发全新的产品线。

Jake: 没错。我们的目标是要把通信带到另一个高度。

Kelly: 如果你们认为今年的成绩已经很好了,那等着看明年吧。

Ned: 好啦,好啦。谢谢你们两位,也谢谢大家。接下来,大家开始庆祝吧!

学习重点

first off 首先

英文里表达"首先；第一；一开始"的说法很多，例如：first、firstly、at first、first of all、in the first place、to begin with、in the beginning 等。

- **First off**, you need to turn on your computer.

  首先，你得先开电脑。

constructive criticism 建设性批评

constructive 表示"有建设性的"，也就是能对事情的改善或发展有所帮助。

- If you are open to it, I would like to give you some **constructive criticism**.

  如果你能接受，我想给你一些建设性的批评。

back to the drawing board 重新设计

字面上是"把产品拿回到制图板上"的意思。用来指先前所制作的东西或所做的事情不够好或失败了，必须"重新开始"。

- We are going to have to take this design **back to the drawing board**. It doesn't work.

  我们将必须重新设计这款产品。这样行不通。

take (something) to the next level
使（某事）往上发展到另一个层次

表示向前迈进或发展到另一个阶段或水平，进入一个崭新的里程。

- We would like to **take** this business relationship **to the next level**.

  我们想使这种贸易关系更上一层楼。

Listening Comprehension

Listen to the conversation and answer the following questions.

1. a. ☐ They made some improvements.
   b. ☐ They filed bankruptcy.
   c. ☐ They lowered the production costs.

2. a. ☐ Digicom.
   b. ☐ Top Flight Airlines.
   c. ☐ ITC.

3. a. ☐ To make sure telecommunications continue to make progress.
   b. ☐ To introduce lots of new and interesting drawings.
   c. ☐ To find out if everyone got some constructive criticism.

4. a. ☐ Sun Tech.
   b. ☐ Digicom.
   c. ☐ ITC.

Unit 01

[Photographs]

1. a. He is wearing a T-shirt.
   b. He is looking for a job.
   c. He is reading a book.
   d. He is wearing a blue tie.

2. a. He is using a laptop.
   b. He is looking for his pen.
   c. He is using a computer.
   d. He is looking at a mirror.

[Question and Response]

1. I've been checking the want ads in the newspaper.
   a. You should try the Internet.
   b. No wonder you are late every day.
   c. That's great. They're friends of mine.

2. What's the best way to find a job?
   a. The Internet is a good place to start.
   b. You can call your father to get another.
   c. It's a long story. Do you have time?

3. I'm looking for something in sales.
   a. You need to call the company up.
   b. Really? I didn't know about know they were coming.
   c. Hey, I just saw a job opening in sales.

4. Have you updated your resume?
   a. Yes, I have. It didn't take long.
   b. Yes, I think that's the correct date.
   c. Oh, no! I forgot to e-mail my friend.

Unit 02

[Photographs]

1. **a. She is a receptionist.**
   b. She is talking on the phone.
   c. He is talking on the phone.
   d. He is having an interview.

2. a. This is a resume.
   b. Someone is reading the newspaper.
   c. This is an insurance Web site.
   d. Someone is looking for a job.

[Question and Response]

1. I'd like to apply for the job.
   a. Please fill in this application.
   b. Go straight and turn right.
   c. Of course. Why not?

2. Have a seat.
   a. Thank you. It'll be nice to sit down.
   b. No thanks. I'm not hungry.
   c. No, I don't. I'm sorry.

3. Excuse me. I have a question.
   a. You can put it over there.
   b. Yes, what can I help you with?
   c. That should be no problem.

4. What should I write here?
   a. Please e-mail me your resume.
   b. Just leave that part blank.
   c. You should call 911.

Unit 03 ·······················
[Photograph]

   a. She is dressed formally.
   b. She is dressed casually.
   c. She is wearing a necklace.
   d. She is carrying a lot of books.

[Listening Comprehension]

1. According to the conversation, what should you NOT do during an interview?

Ans: c

2. What does Dave think Josie should ask about during an interview?

Ans: a

Unit 04 ·······················
[Photograph]

   a. They are having an interview.
   b. They are fighting.
   c. They are watching a movie.

   d. They are reading a newspaper.

[Listening Comprehension]

1. Why did the woman decide to stay in New York?

Ans: a

2. What kind of company did the woman work for?

Ans: c

Unit 05 ·······················
[Listening Comprehension]

1. According to the conversation, what are the company's office hours?

Ans: c

2. What is the woman curious about?

Ans: c

3. What is the base salary for salespeople?

Ans: b

4. What do salespeople have to do to get bonuses?

Ans: a

Unit 06 ·······················
[Photographs]

1. a. He is happy.
   b. He is holding a lot of files.
   c. He is talking to his manager.
   d. He is carrying a shopping bag.

2. a. The man doesn't need any help.

b. The woman is asking for help.

c. The man is laughing at the woman.

d. The woman is offering to help.

[Question and Response]

1. Welcome aboard.

   a. Thanks.
   b. Let's go.
   c. Why not?

2. I'll give you a short tour of the office.

   a. When's lunch?
   b. Well, I am not so sure about that.
   c. Thank you. I'd appreciate that.

3. Where is the marketing department?

   a. It's at the end of the hall.
   b. Turn left at the next traffic light.
   c. Go straight for two blocks.

4. When's lunch?

   a. What would you like to eat?
   b. We can have lunch here.
   c. Lunch is from twelve to one.

Unit 07

[Photographs]

1. **a. Her desk is clean.**
   b. She is not using her computer.
   c. She is calling a customer.
   d. She is writing a note.

2. a. She is reading a book.
   b. She is calling a customer.
   c. She is signing for some supplies.
   d. She is having a meeting with her boss.

[Listening Comprehension]

According to the conversation, what number do you have to press before making a call?

Ans: b

Unit 08

[Photographs]

   a. They are sitting.
   b. They are waving good-bye to each other.
   c. They are exchanging business cards.
   d. They are shaking hands.

2. a. He is looking at his laptop.
   b. He is waiting on the street.
   c. He is having problems with his computer.
   d. He is calling a customer.

3. **a. They are having a meeting.**
   b. They are having a party.
   c. They are looking at the computer.
   d. There are four people in the picture.

Unit 09

[Photographs]

1. a. They are on the street.
   b. They are exchanging business cards.
   c. Both of them are females.
   d. One of them is a female.

2. a. Her hair is long.
   b. She is standing.
   c. She is typing something.
   d. She is looking for something.

[Question and Response]

1. I'm Mike. Nice to meet you.
   a. Nice to meet you, too.
   b. Thank you so much.
   c. Let's go and have lunch.

2. How long have you been here for?
   a. I've been to New York several times.
   b. Not very long. Only a few days.
   c. I don't know where to go.

3. How do you like it so far?
   a. So far, it's been great.
   b. I don't think so.
   c. Well, I'm not so sure about that.

4. Let's have lunch sometime next week.
   a. Exercising is good for you.
   b. Great. Let's go fishing.
   c. Sounds great.

Unit 10

[Photographs]

1. a. All of them are males.
   b. They are having a meeting.
   c. Two of them are standing.
   d. Four of them are sitting.

2. a. It says "calling customers at four p.m."
   b. It says "drinks with partners at four p.m."
   c. It says "calling customers at four a.m."
   d. It says "drinks with partners at four a.m."

3. **a. They are doing some paperwork.**
   b. They are having a party.
   c. They are having a lunch break.
   d. They are using a computer.

Unit 11

[Listening Comprehension]

1. Who is calling?
   Ans: a

2. Who does the caller want to speak to?
   Ans: b

3. Who answers the phone?
   Ans: c

4. What is Sam Palmer's extension?
   Ans: b

Unit 12
[Listening Comprehension]

1. Where does Mr. Willis make his call?

Ans: b

2. Is Mr. Palmer in the office?

Ans: a

3. What does Mr. Willis want to talk about with Mr. Palmer?

Ans: c

4. What is the country code of Australia?

Ans: b

Unit 13
[Listening Comprehension]

1. What happened when the man called Australia?

Ans: a

2. Who made the call for the man?

Ans: b

3. What's the phone number that the man wanted to call?

Ans: b

4. Is the man calling a business?

Ans: a

Unit 14
[Listening Comprehension]

1. What does David give the woman?

Ans: b

2. What will the woman do first?

Ans: a

3. How many e-mails are there in the woman's inbox?

Ans: a

4. What is the last thing they need?

Ans: a

Unit 15
[Listening Comprehension]

1. According to the conversation, is now a good time to invest?

Ans: a

2. What are the two men talking about?

Ans: b

3. What should the man do if he wants to make money quickly?

Ans: a

4. According to the conversation, stocks that go up fast often . . .

Ans: c

Unit 16
[Listening Comprehension]

1. When did Rob read the paper?

Ans: c

2. How many points did the stock market lose?

Ans: a

3. What was Rob going to use the money for?

Ans: b

4. According to the conversation, which of the following statements is correct?

Ans: a

Unit 17 ·····················
[Listening Comprehension]

1. When is the man going to get married?

Ans: b

2. What is the bride's name?

Ans: a

3. Who is the man going to invite?

Ans: b

4. What kind of wedding are they planning?

Ans: a

Unit 18 ·····················
[Listening Comprehension]

1. What did they plan to do this Saturday?

Ans: a

2. Is the baby a girl or a boy?

Ans: b

3. Where are they going to have the baby shower?

Ans: a

4. What is Ed afraid of?

Ans: c

Unit 19 ·····················
[Photographs]

1. a. It's a wedding cake.
   b. It's a birthday cake.

c. There are no candles on it.

2. **a. They are holding a lot of presents.**
   b. They are holding a lot of bags.
   c. They are holding a lot of clothes.
   d. They are holding a lot of files.

Unit 20 ·····················
[Photographs]

1. a. They are having a meeting.
   b. They are unhappy.
   c. They are in a restaurant.
   d. They are teenagers.

2. a. She is a bank teller.
   b. She is a waitress.
   c. She is a secretary.
   d. She is a waiter.

3. a. He is reading a book.
   b. He is reading a menu.
   c. The waitress is helping him.
   d. It's raining.

Unit 21
[Listening Comprehension]

1. Who does Drew call on behalf of?

Ans: a

2. Which of the following statements is NOT correct?

Ans: c

3. When will they meet?

Ans: a

4. What does Susan Goldman want to do?

Ans: c

Unit 22
[Listening Comprehension]

1. Why is Drew calling?

Ans: a

2. According to Drew, what has come up?

Ans: a

3. When is Ms. Gleason free on Monday?

Ans: b

4. What time will Ms. Gleason see Susan on Monday?

Ans: c

Unit 23
[Listening Comprehension]

1. According to the conversation, when did the man place the order?

Ans: b

2. What happened to the order?

Ans: c

3. What does Josie need to do to get to the root of the problem?

Ans: a

4. What happened to sales since the man brought the products in?

Ans: a

Unit 24
[Listening Comprehension]

1. What does Rob want the woman to do?

Ans: b

2. Who does the woman want to send the copy to?

Ans: a

3. What happened to ZPX's order?

Ans: c

4. What does Rob think they should do first?

Ans: a

Unit 25
[Listening Comprehension]

1. What does the man think about his company?

Ans: a

2. What price does the man offer if they consider using cheaper materials?

Ans: c

3. Other than their target price, what does the man think they can meet?

Ans: a

4. What is the final price?

Ans: a

Unit 26 ·················

[Listening Comprehension]

1. Why does the man have all those brochures?

Ans: a

2. When does the man think he can have the brochures distributed?

Ans: b

3. What does the woman think the brochures will make the man look like?

Ans: a

4. What does the woman suggest the man do?

Ans: c

Unit 27 ·················

[Listening Comprehension]

1. What do they want to do as soon as they get back to New York?

Ans: b

2. What are the presents for?

Ans: a

[Question and Response]

1. Thank you for your hospitality these past few days.
   a. It's been our pleasure.
   b. Let me know if you have time.
   c. Really, we should get together sometime.

2. Let's have lunch together.
   a. That's a good question.
   b. Sounds great.
   c. Well, we have to talk about it.

3. We got a little something for your staff.
   a. This is very thoughtful of you.
   b. I can't find your stuff.
   c. We don't have very much stuff.

4. We would like to give you a token of our gratitude.
   a. Let's sit down and talk about it.
   b. Thanks for inviting me.
   c. You didn't need to go to such trouble.

Unit 28 ·················

[Listening Comprehension]

1. What's the message about?

Ans: b

2. Where will Jerry be during that week?

Ans: b

3. Why does Jerry need to go to Washington?

Ans: a

4. When do the doors open?

Ans: c

Unit 29 ·················

[Listening Comprehension]

1. What does Sally Jenkins want to do?

Ans: a

2. What is Sam Palmer going to do in Las Vegas?

Ans: b

3. Will Sam Palmer be traveling alone?

Ans: a

4. What are Sam Palmer's travel dates?

Ans: c

Unit 30 ······················
[Listening Comprehension]

1. Why doesn't the woman go to see her dentist?

Ans: a

2. What does the man suggest?

Ans: c

3. What does the man have to do to help the woman out?

Ans: a

4. Whose call does the woman expect?

Ans: c

Unit 31 ······················
[Listening Comprehension]

1. What does the woman want to do on Friday?

Ans: c

2. What kind of report does the woman need to write?

Ans: c

3. When is the deadline for the woman's report?

Ans: c

4. What will the woman do to finish her report?

Ans: a

Unit 32 ······················
[Listening Comprehension]

1. Why is Sam getting concerned?

Ans: b

2. Why do people see Sam more as a buddy than a boss?

Ans: a

3. What is Sam afraid of?

Ans: c

4. What is Sam going to do?

Ans: a

Unit 33 ······················
[Listening Comprehension]

1. When did Mr. Simpson start work at this company?

Ans: b

2. What does the man want to tell Mr. Simpson?

Ans: a

3. What percent raise will Mr. Simpson get?

Ans: c

4. When will Mr. Simpson get another raise if he keeps up the good work?

Ans: b

Unit 34 ······················
[Listening Comprehension]

1. Why does the man call Sally into his office?

Ans: a

2. What does the man notice?

Ans: a

3. What does the man ask Sally to do?

Ans: b

4. What are bonuses based on?

Ans: b

Unit 35 ·········

[Listening Comprehension]

1. Who has been promoted to manager?

Ans: b

2. Where does Brian have to move?

Ans: b

3. How much time do they have to hire a replacement?

Ans: b

4. What will Brian do with the man's approval?

Ans: a

Unit 36 ·········

[Listening Comprehension]

1. How many years has Amy worked for the company?

Ans: a

2. What kind of company has offered Amy a job?

Ans: b

3. Why does Amy want to resign?

Ans: a

4. When will Amy's resignation be effective?

Ans: b

Unit 37 ·········

[Listening Comprehension]

1. How many years has the man worked for the company?

Ans: b

2. What does the man want to do before he gets too old?

Ans: a

3. What is the man looking forward to ?

Ans: c

4. According to the conversation, what has certainly been appreciated?

Ans: a

Unit 38 ·········

[Listening Comprehension]

1. What is the man not satisfied with?

Ans: b

2. What is one reason Billy is being reprimanded for?

And: b

3. Which of the following statements is true?

Ans: a

4. Who has proof that Billy has misappropriated company funds on several occasions?

Ans: b

Unit 39

[Listening Comprehension]

1. Why does Jake know that Toni is new?

Ans: b

2. Who is going to train Toni?

Ans: b

3. Why is the staff lounge a good place to spend time?

Ans: c

4. What does the staff lounge have?

Ans: a

Unit 40

[Listening Comprehension]

1. Who is being trained?

Ans: b

2. What does Toni have to do first?

Ans: a

3. Why dose Jake call Toni by nine a.m.?

Ans: c

4. When is Jake usually out the door and on the way to his first appointment?

Ans: a

Unit 41

[Listening Comprehension]

1. Who is going to see everything that Toni approves?

Ans: b

2. When does the phone slow down a bit?

Ans: c

3. What is Toni NOT responsible for?

Ans: a

4.What does Toni have to approve?

Ans: a

Unit 42

[Listening Comprehension]

1. What does the man want Toni to do?

Ans: a

2. Who should the e-mail be addressed to?

Ans: a

3. When will the meeting be held?

Ans: b

4. What is the purpose of the meeting?

Ans: b

Unit 43

[Listening Comprehension]

1. According to the conversation, which of following can help the company avoid bankruptcy?

Ans: a

2. What does Adam think can reduce office staff by about twenty percent?

Ans: c

3. Will it be enough to get the company back on track if they lay off twenty percent of the administrative staff?

Ans: a

4. Who does Adam think should
   be laid off?
Ans: c

Unit 44 ·····················
[Listening Comprehension]
1. How long has the woman
   been working at the
   company?
Ans: c

2. How long has it been since the
   woman got a promotion?
Ans: a

3. What will the woman do if she
   changes careers?
Ans: a

4. What did the woman study in
   college?
Ans: b

Unit 45 ·····················
[Listening Comprehension]
1. Why are the employees
   threatening to strike?
Ans: a

2. What percent pay increase will
   the company be able to offer
   right now?
Ans: b

3. Which of the following
   statements is correct?
Ans: b

4. By how much do they plan to
   reduce working hours?
Ans: c

Unit 46 ·····················
[Listening Comprehension]
1. What's the woman's bad
   news?
Ans: c

2. Which companies are
   discussing a merger?
Ans: c

3. When is the woman
   going to make the
   announcement?
Ans: b

4. What has the company been
   experiencing?
Ans: a

Unit 47 ·····················
[Listening Comprehension]
1. What should they do if they
   think a product is inferior?
Ans: a

2. What is important when they're
   marketing?
Ans: c

3. What is good to know?
Ans: a

4. What are they going to do in
   August?
Ans: a

Unit 48 ·····················
[Listening Comprehension]
1. What does the woman
   think are traditional forms of
   advertising?
Ans: c

2. What does the man think is a good way?

Ans: c

3. What kind of an advertising budget do they have for this product?

Ans: a

4. What's good about advertising on the Internet?

Ans: c

Unit 49 ·······················
[Listening Comprehension]

1. What's wrong with the products from Thailand?

Ans: a

2. What products are doing well?

Ans: a

3. What does Josie suggest?

Ans: a

4. What does the man think about Josie's suggestion?

Ans: b

Unit 50 ·······················
[Listening Comprehension]

1. What are they going over?

Ans: a

2. What does the budget proposal include?

Ans: a

3. What do the insurance costs fall under?

Ans: b

4. What percent are these figures over budget?

Ans: c

Unit 51 ·······················
[Listening Comprehension]

1. Since when has the company been privately owned?

Ans: b

2. What do they need to do to avoid finding themselves behind the competition?

Ans: a

3. What can't they do without considerable outside investment?

Ans: a

4. What does the man think is the only way to generate the funds they need?

Ans: b

Unit 52 ·······················
[Listening Comprehension]

1. What does Sam think is the worst-case scenario if they continue as they are?

Ans: a

2. What should they at least continue to do?

Ans: c

3. What does Kelly think is a valuable asset to the company?

Ans: b

4. What might happen if they change their clients' systems every time something new comes along?

Ans: a

Unit 53 ······························

[Listening Comprehension]

1. Which of the following older series are not their best sellers?

Ans: c

2. How many older systems do they have?

Ans: b

3. What would happen if they phased out seven or eight of the older systems?

Ans: b

4. What's not true about phasing out the older systems?

Ans: c

Unit 54 ······························

[Listening Comprehension]

1. What has been causing worldwide instability?

Ans: c

2. Why does the man think they should concentrate on the domestic market?

Ans: a

3. What has happened to most international companies recently?

Ans: a

4. What does the man think about the case?

Ans: a

Unit 55 ······························

[Listening Comprehension]

1. What should they take into consideration?

Ans: b

2. What should they clarify?

Ans: a

3. What was the profit share in the last negotiation?

Ans: b

4. What do they want to beef up?

Ans: c

Unit 56 ······························

[Listening Comprehension]

1. What did they do with the feedback?

Ans: a

2. What company will Sun Tech be working in partnership with next year?

Ans: a

3. What is their goal?

Ans: a

4. Who is the leader in digital telecommunications?

Ans: b